A Fair Cc

Celebrating 100 years of policewomen in Birmingham & the West Midlands

Corinne Brazier and Steve Rice

Note from the authors...

This book is dedicated to all the women who took the first steps in the world of policing, who made it possible for those who followed.

In particular, those who gave up all chance of family life in order to concentrate on the career they loved.

History must remember them.

'You can never tell what a woman will do, or is up to, until you try her in the shafts, and if she does kick over the traces, then fire her, that is what I do here.'

Yours truly,

Chief Constable
Bristol City Police
c1920[1]

About the Authors

Corinne Brazier joined West Midlands Police on February 14th 2005 and has worked in a number of roles across the force in the Criminal Records Bureau (now the Disclosure and Barring Service), the DNA Bureau and Information Management. As the Records Manager from 2007 to 2015, Corinne set up the Information Assurance Team and centralised external storage of records. In this role Corinne took a particular interest in historic records, overseeing a number of digitisation projects. She then became a Demand Champion within the Corporate Asset Management Department, helping to establish requirements and facilitate estate solutions before moving to the West Midlands Police Heritage Project to work on relocating the force's museum. Corinne is married with two children.

Steve Rice joined West Midlands Police on August 15th 1990. Throughout his service he has favoured the uniformed role in response, neighbourhood and partnerships functions and the Contact Management Centre. Steve is married to a police officer who features in the book (Georgina Oakley) and has two children. Several members of his family are in the police service with his brother-in-law and sister-in-law both serving police constables in West Midlands Police. Steve also joined the Heritage Project in 2018.

Both Corinne and Steve volunteered at the force's museum and after uncovering the stories of many of the early women police during a digitisation project in 2015, decided to write this book to coincide with the centenary celebrations of women police in the West Midlands in 2017. All profit from the book sales will go to various women's charities across the West Midlands.

The West Midlands Police Museum at the Lock-up – tickets and info from www.WMPeelers.com

Contents

Foreword

It gives me great pleasure as Chief Constable of the West Midlands Police to write the foreword to this book as we mark one hundred years of women in policing in this area.

Today officers, staff and the public do not give a thought to the fact that women play the very same role as men in policing. Women make up over 30% of the force's officers, 47% of PCSOs, 17% of special constables and 61% of police staff. We have three female Chief Officers including the Deputy Chief Constable and many senior women in police officer and staff roles. Whilst this is nothing less than any civilised society should expect the battle for equality was hard fought.

In 2016 we unveiled an updated Roll of Honour for fallen officers and staff. My attention was drawn to Sergeant Mary Jean Baldwin, the first woman to die as a result of an injury on duty in the region in 1959. Mary Jean's story is detailed in the book but she fell down a flight of stairs breaking her ankle and died as a result of a pulmonary embolism whilst confined to her lodgings. Life was hard for women like Mary and we should never forget their contribution in forging a role for women in policing.

This book describes the journey of female officers across one hundred years alongside the story of the evolution of policing in the area. It tells some incredible personal stories as well as providing an important piece of the social history of this region. I would like to commend

Corinne Brazier and Steve Rice for the painstaking effort they have put into creating this important record and to our volunteers at the West Midlands Police Museums who have ensured the preservation of many historical artefacts that have enabled this story to be told in such detail.

It is of course a story that has not ended. There is still more to be done about gender equality at work, but a tipping point has now been reached. British policing can now stand tall in public service as a solid employer of choice for women and an international focal point for women's roles in policing. I am proud West Midlands Police is a leading player in this work.

Chief Constable Dave Thompson QPM LLB

Introduction

The West Midlands Police is fortunate to have a museum with an incredible collection of historic items and records. The Birmingham based museum originated as a detective training facility run by the late Charles Elworthy and in 1995 relocated to Sparkhill where it was then run by the late Dave Cross. In 2018 the decision was made to relocate the museum again to the Steelhouse Lane Lock-up, where it will be relaunched and become more accessible to the public. It holds many artefacts and records relating to West Midlands Police and its predecessor forces across the West Midlands. Most references to 'the museum' in this book relate to the Birmingham facility. A smaller museum has operated in Coventry Central Police Station since 1959.

The museums hold the following records relevant to this book:

- Personal files going back to the early 1900s - mainly Birmingham City Police, some West Midlands Constabulary, Walsall Borough, Dudley Borough, Wolverhampton Borough, Coventry City Police and Staffordshire County Police
- Personnel ledgers going back to the 1850s – mainly Birmingham City Police, some West Midlands Constabulary, Walsall Borough, Wolverhampton Borough, Coventry City Police and Staffordshire County Police Specials
- Watch Committee and some sub-committee minutes (Birmingham City Police)
- Police Orders for Birmingham City Police from 1839 onwards

'Watch Committee minutes' refer to the Birmingham City Watch Committee (unless otherwise stated), responsible for overseeing and regulating the police and fire brigade, addressing traffic issues in the city, approving transport improvements and regulating all manner of licensing (including taxis, entertainments and public houses).

The Judicial Sub-Committee who sat under the Watch Committee and various other committees are also referenced as issues relevant to policing were discussed. These include the 'Finance and Fire Brigade Committee' and 'Salaries, Wages and Labour Committee' that discussed other matters pertinent to the running of the Birmingham Corporation.

References to 'Police Orders' in this book are Birmingham City Police Orders. These are daily orders that went out to all stations with any information officers needed to be aware of. This could include officers joining or retiring, new legislation or regulations, passing attention needed in particular areas or to specific criminal activity and various other matters.

The vast majority of the records held by the museums are from Birmingham City Police therefore this book primarily focusses on Birmingham. Wherever a force is referred to but not named specifically, this will be Birmingham. We have however tried to include relevant information from the other historic West Midlands forces wherever possible, making it the story of the past one hundred years of female police officers across the West Midlands.

Early Women in the Police

From the beginning of policing in Birmingham in 1839 it seems that the recruitment of female police officers was never considered. Birmingham City Police were not isolated, but in a similar position to the majority of the other UK police forces. It may surprise you to know however that female staff were employed to carry out some element of police duty since the very first days of policing Birmingham. In the 3rd entry from the very first book of Birmingham City Police Orders on

8th November 1939 it is recorded that for each sub-division 'a respectable married woman to reside in each station and section house shall be appointed to search all female Prisoners and cook for the men of each section' for which a regulated allowance would be paid[2].

Matrons were first recruited in July 1895 to look after female prisoners at the Lock-up and later, at court too. Miss Thomas, a former governess, was appointed as the first. The Birmingham Daily Mail from 24th October 1901, with a headline: 'The Lady of the Lock-up', stated Miss Thomas was due to resign her position due to her impending marriage. The article went on to say her friends thought she would only last two days, but that she had defied their expectations by going a full six years. She commented on how prisoners have changed over the years – with quite a number of well-dressed and well-educated women initially, to hardened repeat offenders after the turn of the century. The Chief Constable re-advertised the position in October 1901 with a salary of 20/ per week and he was also asked by the Watch Committee to consider the position of a night matron.[3]

By February 1902 it was decided that the sitting room at the lock-up was to become the matrons' sitting room[4] and in March 1902 a new uniform was agreed – to be obtained at a cost not exceeding £6 per annum.[5] It would appear another Miss Thomas was recruited in the original matron's place - details of her appointment are not held but her resignation is recorded in the Judicial Sub-Committee in July 1904.[6] Her replacement was a Mrs Rebecca Lipscombe.[7]

Watch Committee minutes from November 1914 show that their wages were being increased from 25/- per week to 27/- and an additional part time matron was recruited so that the existing matrons could have one day off per week[8]. These roles were separate to police officers and continued to exist well into the Second World War.

Female attendants (or watchers) were recruited to keep watch in cases of female prisoners who had attempted suicide. They carried out their work either in the police station or the hospital. This work was carried out by police officers in cases where men had attempted suicide.

Female typists and clerks also arrived in the early 1900s – significantly, these were noted in police orders in April 1918 – a full year *after* the first female police officers:

Women Typists etc

As women type and shorthand writing clerks are being introduced in various Departments, the Chief Constable thinks it desirable that Superintendents and others in charge of these Departments should just say a few words of caution to the members of the Departments with regard to treatment of these ladies.

They should be treated with every courtesy and consideration and care should be taken that nothing which might offend them should be said or done.

The Chief Constable knows that the members of the various Departments who have been specially selected for the Departments, are members of the Force entirely to be relied upon, with regard to their discretion.

The presence of Women in the Department makes it still more important that care should be observed with regard to everything which might be said or done in their presence[9].

Women and the Great War

The First World War changed women's lives in profound ways, and the authors believe it brought forward women's employment in roles such as policing, as they entered occupations previously reserved for men. One such pioneer was Edith Smith who was recruited in Grantham at the end of 1915, becoming the UK's first attested policewoman (meaning she had powers of arrest and was sworn in). Edith left the force in 1918 after working seven days a week for two years. Five years later, she took her own life by taking a fatal dose of the pain-killer morphia.[10]

At the onset of war the Birmingham City Police establishment strength was given as 1,431 men however the actual establishment was 1,394. Whilst the reader may think this is only 37 men short upon war being declared, an additional 149 men were soon lent to the Armed Forces to act as drill instructors. A total of 571 would eventually serve in the Armed Forces, sadly 56 were to be killed or died from wounds received during the conflict with the majority still lying in a foreign field. We will go on to see other demands placed on the police and how the authorities tried to fill this vacuum at a time when regular recruitment for the police was suspended.

The British Government put Chief Constables under immense pressure to supply officers to the Armed Forces to serve overseas during World War One, this resulted in a shortage of officers for everyday policing duties. At a 'special' Watch Committee meeting on 7th August 1914 the Chief Constable reported that 87 members of the force were reservists and had been called up to join the colours.[11]

In Birmingham for the most part this void was filled by 'first reserve' police officers and special constabulary which saw a rapid expansion throughout the war.

In a circular to police forces on 15th September 1911 the Home Secretary had recommended the creation of two 'police reserves'; a 'first reserve' consisting of police pensioners and other trained men who would in an emergency be temporarily added to the force as regular paid constables; and a 'second reserve' of fit men registered and ready to be called up in an emergency to act as special constables.

Interestingly the 1916 Police Act makes reference to 'fit men' becoming constables but the Special Constables Act 1831 only specified fit 'persons'. The Chief Constable of Gloucester decided to exploit this in 1918 by recruiting women as special constables and then swearing them in as full members of the force.[12]

The first police reserve was called up on the declaration of war and many of them were still serving in 1919. This reserve of retired officers was also heavily utilised during the Second World War and for a number of years thereafter. The second reserve formed the nucleus of the special constabulary during the war which gradually increased in size and efficiency, allowing the release of many of the regular constables to join the Armed Forces. The Home Office wrote again to forces in January 1919 stating how important it was for these reserve forces to be retained during peace time, to be called upon during the event of any future emergency. The special constabulary would have less work imposed on them as regular officers returned from the Armed Forces, but they would remain a vital part of the workforce.[13]

There were reports of moral and social decline in Birmingham at the start of the war. An article in the Birmingham Post in 1914 stated soldiers' wives in receipt of a separation allowance from the Government were spending far too much of their time and money in the pub. The article stated the situation was 'depraving to the women, bad, unutterably bad in its effects upon their children and home life generally'[14].

The First Women Police

In the early 20th century there were a large number of organisations campaigning for women's suffrage and women's rights. Some significant ones in relation to the campaign for women police are the Women's Social and Political Union (WSPU), the Women's Labour League (WLL), The National Council of Women (formerly known as the National Union of Women Workers, NCW or NUWW) and the National British Women's Temperance Association (NBWTA).

By 1914 the suffragettes were becoming increasingly aggressive and vandalising government buildings. The outbreak of war crucially stopped this activity from escalating even further as a truce was called with the Government and suffragettes were released from prison. This gave them the opportunity to contribute to the war effort and demonstrate the value of women when given the same opportunities as men, at a time the country most needed it.

Shortly after war broke out, the first organisations specifically set up with the ambition of employing women in policing were created.

Nina Boyle

Constance Antonia 'Nina' Boyle was born in 1865 and spent time working in hospitals in South Africa during the Boer War. She returned to England in 1911 and immediately set about campaigning for women's rights. Nina saw the campaign for mass recruitment of special constables as an opportunity for women to play their part in policing during the war, but the Home Office was not supportive and it wasn't until 1918 that women were recruited as special constables. Instead she set about recruiting women police herself.[15]

Margaret Damer-Dawson

A charismatic and wealthy philanthropist, Margaret was born in 1873. Prior to the First World War she was awarded medals in Finland and Denmark for her campaigning for animal rights[16] and received the OBE in 1918. She also sought to recruit 'women police' shortly after the outbreak of war. She quickly heard about Nina Boyle's plans and the pair joined forces, so as not to overlap their intentions and as the old saying goes, to achieve 'strength in numbers'.

Commandant Margaret Damer-Dawson (left) and second-in-command Mary Allen

Mary Sophia Allen

Born in 1878, Mary was a quiet girl with an affluent upbringing. She became involved in suffragette activity in 1908 and was a member of the WSPU. Her father disagreed vehemently with their activities and instructed her to desist her involvement or leave his house. She chose the latter. After completing her third prison sentence and increasingly longer and more painful prison hunger strikes (the prison authorities quickly decided to force feed those on hunger strike, rather than simply release them which had been their first course of action) she was told to take a less active role in the organisation and became more of a planner and organiser.

The Voluntary Women's Patrols and the Women Police Service

There were two main organisations promoting the role women could play in policing by the end of 1914:

- The Voluntary Women Patrols (chaired by the Women's Patrol Committee), organised by the National Council of Women. This consisted of more affluent women, prepared to work locally for a few hours a week. They had no uniform but wore an armlet supplied by the local police force. They had the support of the Metropolitan Police Commissioner and the Home Office.
- The other was the Women Police Volunteers (WPV) – created by Nina Boyle and Margaret Damer-Dawson. These women were full time and wanted powers of arrest. They were issued with a uniform and went anywhere they were sent. Initially these women were also supported by the Commissioner and the Home Office.

The work for both organisations generally consisted of trying to address the significant problems of 'immorality' and prostitution going on in the streets and near army bases. The public were demanding that the police do something to 'clean up the streets' and several police forces saw that women could help to address this problem.

In February 1915 Nina Boyle and Margaret Damer-Dawson argued over some of the work being carried out by the WPV which led to a vote by the members over the way forward – Miss Damer-Dawson won by a landslide and Miss Boyle subsequently left the organisation.[17]

Miss Damer-Dawson took control and renamed the group the Women Police Service. Mary Allen was her second in-command and the two were very close. Women were recruited and trained with the ambition of providing competent female officers to the early forces looking to recruit women police officers and also to the fairly significant war duties undertaken during the Great War by women. This included female munitions police who undertook security and general policing duties in munitions factories. Later confusion between this organisation and women officers from the Metropolitan Police Service (who started in 1918) led to them being renamed the Women's Auxiliary Service.[18]

King George V and Princess Mary inspecting the munitions police in Gretna, 1917, courtesy of the Devil's Porridge Museum

The Police Act 1916 actually made provision for 'women patrols' (albeit not women police officers). When this act was passed the Metropolitan Commissioner immediately set about recruiting Special Patrols who were to be accompanied by a police constable.

In 1918 the newly appointed Commissioner, General Sir Nevil Macready created the Metropolitan Women Police department, an official branch of women police within the force. The first recruits consisted mainly of former Women Patrols and only one member of the WPS, an organisation which this Commissioner disliked.

When Damer-Dawson died unexpectedly in 1920, Mary Allen took control of the WPS and later became somewhat of an ambassador for the British policewoman around the world.

Mary Allen (left) and Margaret Damer-Dawson – photo courtesy of Joan Lock

Bristol Training School

The Bristol Training School also played a significant role in the training of women to be deployed in police forces and munitions factories across the country during this time period. It was set up by the Bristol branch of the VWP in 1915 to train women in police duties and ran  short courses for the patrols and longer courses for the women police. Right from the start they were told they had to keep patrols and police officers separate. They also trained hundreds of female munitions police. Dorothy Peto was a founding member and initially had the role of assistant to the director. She took charge herself when the director left in 1917. In 1918 she also took on responsibility for the Glasgow and Liverpool training schools.

Flyer for the Bristol Training School showing 'The Director' - Miss Dorothy Peto

Birmingham Chief Constable Charles Haughton Rafter found the Bristol training school quite lacking – in a letter to a potential candidate for recruitment he states:

'It will be necessary, if you join this Police Force, that you go through a course in the Police School, and also a course with the Detectives...

It was quite apparent that the Bristol Police
Training School was not qualified to impart
instruction in Police duties; those in charge of
the school not being competent to impart training in
Police Duties.'[19]

The Campaign for Women Police in Birmingham

During the early part of the war the National Council of Women's
Birmingham Branch campaigned to reduce the opening hours of local
public houses in Birmingham and was approached by various people
and organisations and asked to set up a patrol committee to address
urgent need for work amongst young girls. They promptly organised a
Women's Patrol Committee in November 1914, who recruited women
to patrol the streets and try to provide alternative 'safe entertainment
for working class women'. The Central Committee for Patrol Work sent
Miss Boutchard to train women who wanted to work as patrols. The
women received 'instruction in police control and in methods of girl
life', wore an armband and carried a card of authority issued by the
Chief Constable.[20] These women could be considered the forerunners
of policewomen in Birmingham.

Miss Boutchard's report from November 1914 details her early
experiences in Birmingham – trying to recruit volunteers, meeting with
the Chief Constable and trying to locate suitable premises to set up the
girls' club. She refers to her first meeting with the Chief Constable:

'When Mrs Ashley and I reached the Chief Constable's
office, we found Alderman Sayer with him and both
entered cordially into our business.

Mr Rafter signed my card and answered all my questions as to streets and hours. The subject of counter-attractions was touched upon and the importance of being able to offer the girls a fresh suggestion – if possible, something connected with our soldiers and sailors.

Alderman Sayer at once offered some empty premises of his, both fairly central, and suggested that one of the things which would be really useful, and likely to attract the class of girl we have in our minds, would be to offer to mend the socks of the men quartered in the town.'[21]

The committee were based at 10 Easy Row, Birmingham. By December 1914, 20 patrols had been established and by March 1915 a grand total of 35, although eight had been forced to give it up for various reasons.

The women worked through a bad winter and reportedly got along well with all authorities, civic and military with no friction.

Most of the patrol work was outside barracks at Thorpe Street, but also around Moseley College where couples were frequenting (extra police supervision was secured) and near Witton cemetery. At Thorpe Street barracks many girls were often waiting outside as early as 6am, always about during dinner and tea, hoping to catch the attention of the soldiers.

The police reportedly saw the value of the patrols and were very sympathetic to their work. One example was given of a PC asking the patrols to speak to a young girl in the hope that it would have a better effect than an official police warning asking her to move on. The Patrol Committee organiser's report from March 1915[22] stated:

'This puts very clearly one great argument for permanent women patrols, and also defined to some extent their proper relation to the Police authorities.'

From the valuable experience they had gained during the last few months, and from the excellent results achieved, the committee felt that they may put forward a strong recommendation for the appointment of paid, permanent women police, in place of the voluntary patrols.

The report for the week ending Jan 30th (presumably in 1915) by Helen Wright highlights:

'Work has been done around Thorpe Street Barracks and Curzon Hall during time that entertainment for soldiers was on. Some nights it is very quiet but some nights there are many rowdy girls. The women patrols have been supplying information to the Clerk to the Licensing Justices about drinking going on in Thorpe Street, who was glad to hear the information. He is able to act upon the information without bringing in the name of the patrols.[23]'

With less soldiers around by March 1915 the work was winding down but the women were told to remain ready for rapid mobilisation should a large number of soldiers return.

The Patrol Committee also ran the Girls' Patriotic Club which had a valuable service in providing a place for girls to go and learn new skills and not be outside on the streets, subjected to the 'moral dangers' of so many young soldiers.

Mrs Barrow Cadbury kindly located a premises and provided the first 3 months' rent and some furniture for the rooms and the Girls Club went from strength to strength.

In April 1915 the Women's Patrol Committee were confident enough in their work to approach the Birmingham Watch Committee about the issue of permanent women police officers. Records from the Watch Committee's Judicial Sub-Committee in April 1915 state:

'A letter was read from the Women's Patrol Committee urging the appointment of Women Police. This was considered by the committee and resolved stating that the Committee be informed that this Sub Committee do not consider that there is any need in Birmingham at present for the appointment of Women Police.'[24]

To the reader this may be considered a little short sighted however there is a need to consider the general optimism of the time that this war would be a short lived conflict and those officers that had gone to war would soon return. Few would have believed the reality; that this was a new type of war that was to be fought on an industrial scale. The flesh of men was pitted against the rapid fire of modern weapons and high explosive artillery shells. The war dragged on through 1915 into 1916 and through the carnage of the Somme offensive between 1st July and the 18th November. During those few months there were over 420,000 British casualties. More men were needed and the Home Office put pressure on police forces throughout the country to provide more men for the Army. In addition to those who joined the Army, almost 100 officers were 'loaned' into agriculture to work the fields to replace the workers who had joined the colours to fight for their country.

The National British Women's Temperance Association, another women's rights organisation to approach the Judicial Sub-Committee on the matter of women police, were pushing for the police to enhance their numbers with women police, particularly to deal with women and children. In July 1915 a deputation was received:

'A deputation from the National British Women's Temperance Association attended the Sub Committee on the question of the appointment of women police. The deputation stated their views on the matter and urged the Watch Committee to appoint women police with a view particularly of dealing with the cases of women and girls and advertisements, and exercising supervision in Theatres, Picture houses, Massage establishments, Common Lodging Houses, and such other places or ground not covered by Policemen'.[25]

The chairman informed the deputation that the sub-committee would give consideration to the matter, and the deputation withdrew. The Chief Constable was requested to obtain information with regard to the work of women police in other towns, so that the matter could be further considered in due course.

This would seem an appropriate time to reference the Chief Constable at the time – Sir Charles Haughton Rafter, who led the Birmingham City Police through the Great War and oversaw the appointment of the first female officers in the West Midlands. Formerly of the Royal Irish Constabulary, he was appointed Chief Constable of Birmingham City Police in 1899 and in 1909 he was awarded the Kings Police Medal.

He was commended for his tact and integrity during the First World War, giving early instructions under the Defence of the Realm Regulations in November 1914 for the city to extinguish its lights upon air raid alarms being sounded. This was criticised for being overzealous at the time, however by January 1916 when the Zeppelin bombers came over the Midlands – Birmingham was left unscathed whereas in the Black Country less than 10 miles away, where no similar precautions had been instructed, German Zeppelins struck and several people were killed and many injured.[26]

In 1920 he was made Commander of the Most Excellent Order of the British Empire and in 1927 was made Knight Commander of the same order. He possessed excellent organisational qualities and was described as a man who had a deep understanding of human nature. Undoubtedly these qualities are the reason for the force to be rated as having a very high standard of efficiency at that time. In 1924 on the occasion of completing 25 years with the force he was presented with a life size painting in oils (seen here on the left) which the museum are very proud to have in the collection.

By May 1916 the matrons at the lock-up were granted a war bonus of 2/- per week[27]. Records show the matrons at this time were:

- Mrs S A Evans
- Mrs R Lipscombe
- Miss A Bird

- Mrs Thomas (part-time – only received 1/- per week war bonus)

In December 1916 the Judicial Sub-Committee accepted the resignation of Mrs Evans, who had received a disablement in the service of the corporation and was granted a gratuity payment accordingly, and in the same meeting resolved that Mrs Thomas (existing part-time matron and widow of Inspector Thomas) be appointed as a full-time matron and that Mrs Evelyn Miles (wife of police pensioner ex-Sergeant Miles) be appointed part-time matron. [28]

At this time the National Council of Women were still campaigning for female police officers to be recruited in Birmingham – following the likes of other police forces such as Liverpool and Southampton[29]. Together with the Women's Labour League and the Women's Co-operative Guild they had petitioned hard throughout 1915 and 1916.

By April 1917, the Judicial Sub-Committee received another deputation on the subject of women police including two members of the Cadbury family (Mrs Barrow Cadbury and Councillor Mr Cadbury). They urged the appointment of women police, particularly to deal with cases involving women and children. The Chief Constable was again requested to communicate with police forces in other towns where women police were already in existence and report back to the sub-committee as soon as possible.[30]

When the Judicial Sub-Committee next sat at the end of April 1917 it was requested that a special sub-committee be set up to specifically consider the appointment of women police. It was requested that the Lord Mayor, Alderman James and Sanders, Councillors T. Brown and Heath were on the committee.[31]

On the 14th May 1917 both the Judicial Sub-Committee and the Watch Committee discussed the appointment of women police with the former recommending it and the latter accepting the recommendation.

At the Watch Committee meeting on that day it was decided that Mrs Rebecca Lipscombe and Mrs Evelyn Miles be appointed as the city's

first policewomen and that the Chief Constable should set out exactly what duties they would perform. Their starting salary was set at 35/- per week and they were to be issued with a uniform.

Evelyn Miles and Rebecca Lipscombe, Birmingham Weekly Mercury 9th June 1917

Two further matrons were requested to replace them and a further matron was to be appointed, to be present in court for all cases concerning women or children [32]. Both women's records show they started as women police on the 30th April 1917, meaning the decision was backdated by two weeks.

At 35/- per week they earned 10/- more per week than they did as lock-up matrons. It is difficult to compare exactly with male officers as there were no male officers recruited during the First World War but by way of example:

- The last male officer recruited prior to the war in 1914 started on 27/- per week
- The next male officer recruited after the war in 1919 started on 70/- per week (showing a huge inflation in wages post war following the 1918 and 1919 police strikes)

By July 1917 the Chief Constable was able to report on the duties carried out by the women police and asked that the various women's organisations that had campaigned for their introduction, help to address the social issues identified in the many cases the women police were now dealing with.[33]

In August 1917 the topic of the war bonus paid to members of the force was discussed in relation to the female officers and the matrons and this was subsequently raised from 2/- to 5/- per week.[34] This leaves a clear distinction between the matrons and women police, and the other female members of the force – the cleaners, cooks and female searchers.

The casualties from the war were starting to add up now and a report to the Judicial Sub-Committee in October 1917 shows that of the men who had left the force to join the armed forces, 28 were dead, 47 wounded, one missing and five were prisoners of war. It was at this point that the Chief Constable recommended recruiting a third policewoman and had clearly given the matter some thought already as a Mrs Malinda Shawe was immediately recommended for appointment during the same meeting, also on 35/- per week.[35]

The strain on the force from the war was not limited to men who had left to join the armed forces. Men were also offered the chance to support farmers with agricultural work. In October 1917 it was reported that of the 98 men who had been released for agricultural work, 89 were still engaged on that work and the farmers wanted them to remain. The issue of pay had come up however as a policeman's wage was better than that of an agricultural worker and the Watch Committee decided that the farmers would only be allowed to have the officers continue to work on their farms if they increased their wages from 25/- to 35/-[36] (the same as the female officers, but still less than their male counterparts would have received for police work).

In the middle of October 1917, the Birmingham Joint Executive of the Women's Co-operative Guild wrote to the Judicial Sub-Committee, urging the appointment of further women police. They highlighted the successful work already done (in the space of five months) and requested that the Watch Committee increase the numbers of women police.[37] The Guild were informed that their request would receive the consideration of the Watch Committee, who would 'augment the numbers, as the occasion requires.'

The question of increasing the number of women police would appear to have already been under consideration by the Watch Committee as by the end of October 1917 a further two women had been recruited. Miss Elsie Chapman and Mrs Mary Dwelly.

Wolverhampton – First Female Specials

It is believed that Wolverhampton Borough Police have the accolade of recruiting the first female special constables in England and Wales. On 2nd July 1917 Chief Constable David Webster asked the Watch Committee to recruit female special constables, to help fill the gap made by male officers joining the Forces. The request was made for women to specifically 'patrol on the street, or to do any other duty such as visiting public parks, theatres and particularly working amongst their own sex and juveniles'.[38] Permission was granted and the names of those pioneer special constables are reproduced in a beautiful illuminated volume created by Violet Clinton, of the Wolverhampton School of Art, held within the City Archives:

Hilda Hutchinson Smith	Lillie Highfield-Jones M.B.E.	Carmen Buchanan
Sylvia May Sankey	Muriel Elsie Hobbs	Elsie Leonora Corbett
Lilian Manley	Gertrude Buxton Matthews	Doris M. Mulliner
Florence I. Manley	Lizzie Brookes	Catherine B. Thomson
Sarah A. Tonks	Jane Buckley	Elizabeth Shingler
Lilian Humphreys	Ida Robinson	Susan Parker
May Nickless	Agnes Eason	Phillis Killin
Kathleen Smith	Doris Higgs	Mary Hanmer
Gladys M. Hill	Janet Killin	Dorothy Sargent (deceased)
Amy E. Lockwood		

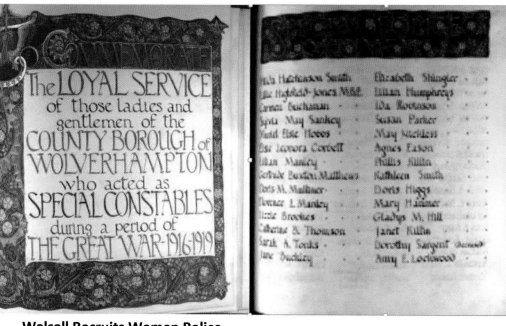

The LOYAL SERVICE of those ladies and gentlemen of the COUNTY BOROUGH of WOLVERHAMPTON who acted as SPECIAL CONSTABLES during a period of THE GREAT WAR·1916-1919

Walsall Recruits Women Police

Walsall was not far behind Birmingham and became the first force in the Black Country to recruit female police officers. The first two arrived in May 1918 – Miss Katherine Mary Tearle and Miss Williams had worked as munitions police in Herefordshire and Gretna – Miss Tearle having also worked as a sergeant. The Watch Committee were asked to approve their salary of 36/ a week (one shilling more than Mrs Miles and Mrs Lipscombe of 35/ per week) with a slightly higher war bonus of 10/ per week, and it was decided they would work on the same terms as their male colleagues[39]. These pictures are of Sergeant Tearle and Miss Williams, whilst working as munitions police in 1917. Little is known about Miss Williams but we know Miss Tearle earned her sergeant's stripes in Walsall by August 1918. It would seem she had left by 1919 as she returned home to Bisham to marry Charles Leonard

Randall, a farmer. They do not appear to have had any children and Katherine died in 1967[40].

These pictures are of Sergeant Tearle and Miss Williams, Munitions Police at one of HM Factories in Hereford 1917. They are believed to be the same Miss Tearle and Miss Williams who went on to be the first women police in Walsall.

Key National Developments for Women Police

The Government attitude towards women police was indecisive – when women complained that most female officers were not attested, many forces stated they were waiting for advice from the Home Office on the matter. In 1919 a circular was issued from the Home Office to all Chief Constables in England and Wales advocating the benefits of women police officers to undertake police duties but stated that they need not be sworn in.[41]

The Desborough Committee was set up by the Government in May 1919 with a purpose of considering the requirements of police forces across England and Wales. The Federated Training Schools for women police of Bristol, Liverpool and Glasgow petitioned the committee to be allowed to give evidence on the pay and conditions of women police. This was denied as they felt it was not in their terms of reference – indeed they refused to minute any approval or thoughts on the position of women police at all.[42]

The Home Secretary was then asked to consider the role of women police and to set up a further committee on this subject. In his reply, Mr Edward Shortt indicates the Government appreciated the value of women police but was cautious in considering their expansion. Upon a further deputation being received by the Home Secretary which highlighted the uncertain conditions for women police and their poor pay and lack of prospects, a committee was promised the following year to deliberate the matter further.[43]

Following relentless campaigning by various women's organisations, the Sex Disqualification Act 1919 was passed. Significantly this did not allow for a woman to be 'disqualified by sex or by marriage from the exercise of any public function'.

In 1920 when the Baird Committee on Women Police was set up – its seven members included two women – Dame Helen Gwynne-Vaughan, the female controller in chief of the Women's Auxiliary Air Force and Lady (Nancy) Astor the first female to sit in the House of Commons as a Member of Parliament (who was only able to stand for election in 1919 following the new legislation on gender discrimination). Constance Markievicz was actually the first female MP to be elected but refused to take her seat. She was a member of Sinn Fein and all Sinn Fein MPs refused to come to Westminster, albeit they were elected to Parliament. Constance was elected in 1918 following her role in the 1916 Easter Rising and she did not take up where a husband had left off.

Nancy Astor (left) and Constance Markievicz

It is interesting to note that at this point even though women were starting to be elected as members of parliament, only women over 30 who were householders were allowed to vote – it would be another eight years before women over 21 were given the right to vote.

Assistant Secretary Harry Butler Simpson from the Home Office was one of the first witnesses to give evidence to the committee. He outlined the definition of a policeman and the development of the role of an officer. He referred to the effectiveness of a policeman being down to the 'prestige his behaviour had gained him, a very handy weapon which he had to assist him, but, not least, to his superior physical strength – superior that is to the average law-breaker, who was not likely to know about the constable's special powers of arrest and be influenced by them; thus it was pointless giving these powers to women.' Dame Helen questioned him as to whether the handy weapon could be employed by women also, and received the following reply: 'I would hope that women should be so employed that they would not have to come into actual physical conflict with malefactors.'[44] One wonders what he would have made of female officers today and the variety of kit they are equipped with.

Sir Charles Haughton Rafter attended and gave evidence of the social work carried out by the women police in Birmingham. He was one of the first Chief Constables to be supportive of the need for female officers and he was really starting to experience their value.

One should also not underestimate the women patrols - Mrs Florence Young was called to give evidence about her patrols operating in Bristol. Their use of ju-jitsu was questioned:

'616 You would rely on the use of ju-jitsu I understand?

Yes I could easily get a man down and sit on him.

617 If nobody came along for a considerable time you might have to sit there for a long time?

Yes I think one could do so and still keep him in agony.' [45]

The recommendations included women to be attested and given full power of arrest, to deal with all matters involving women or children and for their pay to be increased to 60/- per week. The age of entry was to be 25-30 years (extended for the first five years to cater for women with police or HM Forces service during the war)[46].

Whilst the Police Federation supported a ban on marriage as they felt a married woman's primary obligations should be to her children and that it would be unfair for married women to compete with single women for jobs, as the latter had no husband to support them,[47] it was felt that there was insufficient evidence to make any recommendations on the topic of marriage at this stage.

The Home Office apparently gave little credence to the findings and recommendations of the Baird Committee – the report was sent to all constabularies with an accompanying Home Office circular advising forces to ignore the recommendations about better pay and powers of arrest.[48]

Home Office regulations based on these recommendations were not to come for a further 11 years.

The First Female Police Officers in Birmingham

When Mrs Rebecca Lipscombe and Mrs Evelyn Miles were appointed as the first uniformed female officers for Birmingham City Police in 1917, neither of these women were attested. Therefore their only power of arrest was under common law, which provided for anyone to make an arrest of an individual under the Vagrancy Act 1824, The Highways Act of 1835, larceny offences and for indictable offences between the hours of 9:00pm and 6:00am![49]

Rebecca was almost 61 and Evelyn was 54 when they were appointed - they certainly started their new career at a late stage in their lives!

On the 8th October 1917 Mrs Malenda Shaw (spelt as per personnel ledger, although Watch Committee minutes state Melinda Shawe) was appointed, following approval at the Judicial Sub-Committee on 1st October 1917[50]. Her file has unfortunately not survived.

Personnel ledgers at the force museum show that Miss Elsie Chapman was appointed on the 24th September 1917 as a 'court matron' on 25/- per week (10/- less than Evelyn and Rebecca). Interestingly on the back of her summary sheet, on the date she was appointed it states:

'Miss Chapman will perform duty in the dock whenever female prisoners are brought up, but will be available for any other duty either as Policewoman or Matron as necessary.'[51]

This shows real forward thinking from the Chief Constable and the Watch Committee as it would be another 16 years before legislation was passed requiring a female officer to be in court for all cases concerning children.

Mrs Dwelly followed in October 1917. Neither her file nor Miss Chapman's has survived.

Watch Committee minutes from 31st October 1917[52] confirm that Miss Elsie Chapman was engaged to perform police duty from 24th September 1917 with wages of 25/- per week but that Miss Chapman and Mrs Dwelly (note originally recorded as Dively, but crossed out and corrected to Dwelly) were subsequently appointed as additional women police with wages of 35/- per week. Miss Chapman's record in the personnel ledger however indicates she remained at 25/- until 1926 when her wages and war bonus were amalgamated to 39/- per week – she seems to have remained primarily as a court matron, thus her lower salary.

Lizzie May Peers joined in September 1918 but her file has not survived either. Lucy Charlton joined on the same day and her file is still held by the museum.

Police Orders from 1919[53] show Police Woman Mary Dwelly resigned on the 27th April 1919 at her own request, becoming the first female policewoman in Birmingham to resign. Lizzie May Peers followed in December 1919 and Malenda Shaw in 1922.

The research for the first edition of this book allowed us to pinpoint the year of this picture – 1919 – and confirm it as the only known group picture of the early Women Police Department, with all those recruited up to 1920 (with no more being recruited until 1931). Following publication we were able to positively identify the lady standing on the left as Lizzie May Peers, who later emigrated to Canada.

Standing L to R   1) Lizzie May Peers   2) Lucy Charlton   3) Catherine Downey   4) Sarah Hancox   5) Ellen Vernon   6) Not identified
Seated L to R   1) Not identified   2) Sergeant Evelyn Miles   3) Adelaide Pearce

Of the two that remain unconfirmed - we believe the lady standing on the right is Malenda Shawe, as she appears on patrol in another picture held in the archives, which would make sense with Malenda staying longer than the only other potential candidate. This leaves the other female officer (seated on the left) as being Mary Dwelly.

Mrs Rebecca Lucy Lipscombe could technically be referred to as the first female officer in Birmingham as her name appears first on the Watch Committee minutes. Unfortunately her file has not survived but there is an entry about her in a personnel ledger which states she was born on the 23rd May 1856 and she joined Birmingham City Police as a lock-up matron in April 1904.

Her marriage certificate shows Rebecca's maiden name was Allen and baptism records show she had a son, Gabriel, who was baptised on March 28th 1877. No father's name is recorded and she is shown as a single woman who resided in the workhouse. She married Thomas Lipscombe (who was 10 years her junior) in 1891 when she was 32. In the 1901 census she is living with Thomas and her son (who still has the surname Allen, aged 24) who was recorded as the step-son of the head of the household (Thomas Lipscombe).

This picture of a matron in the Central Lock-up is believed to be Rebecca:

Whilst Mrs Miles went on to be promoted to sergeant in July 1918, Mrs Lipscombe's record shows she reverted back to being a lock-up matron in March 1918 (which paid 8/- a week less than a female police officer). Her record doesn't indicate when she eventually left the force but the last entry on her sick record is from November 1932 to January 1933 when she would have been almost 77 years of age. Whilst Evelyn Miles is fairly well documented as the first female police officer in the Midlands, very little has been recorded about Rebecca Lipscombe – possibly because of her very short service as a police officer.

Mrs. Evelyn. Miles.

Mrs Miles' personal file shows she officially started as a police officer on the 30th April with previous service as a lock-up matron. Her personal file shows she was born in Cirencester on 27th September 1867 and she is recorded as being 5 foot 4 inches tall.

Her birth certificate however indicates she was born Mary Eveline Radway in 1862 – meaning she changed her name and made herself five years younger than she really was when she applied to join the police.

In the 1881 census her age is recorded as 18, she has a four month old son (George Radway) and is living with an uncle. She married her husband Walter Robertson Miles in 1885 and George takes his name by the 1891 census. Interestingly it would also seem that both Walter and Evelyn were children born to unwed mothers.

The 1901 census records that Evelyn and Walter had two boarders – 32 year old medical student Charles H G Atkyns, and a 14 year old servant

– Agnes Durham. One year old Winifred Adams is also resident with the family. She was born in Birmingham and adopted by the Miles family.

The 1911 census shows Evelyn as living with Walter, 11 year old Winifred and a servant Clara Allaway (aged 20) – Evelyn is now recorded as being 50.

Documentation from October 1916 indicates that Mrs Miles applied for the position of lock-up matron which she had heard may shortly become vacant and that she was the wife of ex-PS Walter Miles who was employed in the Explosives Department, but owing to ill-health was 'removed to the City Asylum in Winson Green' in 1913 where he was still an inmate. Entries on personnel ledgers from the 1800s show he joined Birmingham City Police aged 29 in 1890, having previously served in the Gloucestershire Constabulary. Unusual for the time, his records show no misconduct or disciplinary issues. The majority of officers had some form of disciplinary issues recorded – common offences being neglecting or being absent from their beat or being drunk on duty. After being transferred to the Explosives Department in 1903, he eventually left due to ill-health on the pay of a 4th class sergeant of 38/- a week. The Watch Committee granted him a medical pension on the 15th October 1913. By the time Mrs Miles had joined the force he is referred to as 'the late Sergeant Miles'.

Correspondence submitted to the Chief Constable stated that Mrs Miles was well known to members of the force as a 'very highly respected woman' who had been housekeeper to a local doctor for many years. In December 1916 she was appointed an assistant matron at the lock-up.

She had a respectable sick record for her 22 years' service (especially considering she was 77 when she retired). This includes eight counts of bronchitis, one of asthma, one of a sore throat and she once reported sick with a septic arm which she required 29 days off for in 1933. Her records show she had a fall when coming on duty whereby she injured her left elbow and broke the skin.

During 1930 Mrs Miles covered the work of the lady enquiry officer from the Criminal Investigation Department (CID) when they went on leave. This work was separate to the work of the uniformed Women Police Department that was run by Mrs Miles. The CID first recruited a female enquiry officer in 1919.

In December 1939 Mrs Miles' health was deteriorating (although admirably she had only taken one day off sick since February 1938) and the force surgeon recommended she be retired from the force as she was suffering from bronchitis, emphysema and cardiac weakness.

In an interview with the Birmingham Post on January 2nd 1940[54] (two days after her retirement) she said the early days of her work were very difficult indeed and she suffered a lot of jeering from both men and women. She goes on to say that 'she continued her work long enough to see virtually all prejudice against women police vanish from Birmingham'. This point is debatable, particularly as it wasn't until 1946 that the ban on marriage was lifted and much later that women were starting to be represented in all areas of policing. Women also felt under a lot of pressure to leave the police if they had a child – it remained uncommon right up to the 1980s for women to return after maternity leave and continue with police work.

Mrs Miles stated that her only regret was that she didn't begin her work sooner.

She died in 1954 aged 91. Based on the birth date on her birth certificate – she is believed to hold the record for the oldest serving female officer in the West Midlands at aged 77.

Both Mrs Miles and Mrs Lipscombe showed immense strength of character to have gone from being young, unwed mothers to respectable married ladies, considered suitable for employment in the police force – where a good reputation was vital and a hint of scandal could see you sacked.

Charlton Lucy Agnes

It was November 1917 when Lucy Charlton first applied to become a Birmingham City police officer. She stated she had served 10 years in the Prison Service but had left two and a half years earlier to marry the prison warder, and she was 37 years of age. She was informed that there were not currently any vacancies, but that they would bear her application in mind if there were any in future.

She was eventually able to join in September 1918, on the same day as Lizzie Peers.

The chaplain from Winson Green prison where she had worked as a prison officer wrote a lovely testimonial, stating she was a strong character, of good moral tone, tactful and active and he could hardly think of a more suitable woman to become a policewoman.

In December 1937 she had an accident when alighting from an omnibus on Steelhouse Lane – the omnibus started before she had fully disembarked, leading to her falling heavily on her ankle and dislocating it. After a four month battle, including a few months of light duties and removal from street patrolling, the claim against the Birmingham Corporation due to negligence by the omnibus driver was settled in her favour and she was awarded £30 in settlement of her claim with £51.9.11 going to the Watch Committee for their loss in paying her wages for the time she could not work.

In 1940 she wrote to ask permission to reside at the residence of her niece slightly outside the city boundaries in West Bromwich due to her house in Handsworth receiving extensive damage from enemy action.

In November 1942, she received a certificate from the force doctor, who recommended a medical retirement, owing to her experiencing chronic arthritis in both knees.

She left the force in December 1942, aged 62. In October 1944 the Chief Constable wrote to her enquiring if she would like to fill a vacancy as a matron at the lock-up! She replied that unfortunately her knees were still giving her trouble and she did not think she could fulfil the role, not least because of all the stairs to climb.

Vernon   Ellen Sarah

Four other women were appointed in January 1919 – the first, Ellen Vernon aged 52, was the widow of a music teacher. She actually lied about her age when she first requested an application form in April 1918 – she stated she was 45 when she was actually 51. Enquiries into her character revealed she had been widowed about two years previously and had two children: one who was married and working as an electrician, and a daughter who was an invalid and lived in Leamington. She had recently been carrying out government inspection work at a factory but left as she did not like being in the factory and wanted to work outside.

There is one serious illness recorded in her file: in 1924 she called in sick and when the doctor visited her at her home address he found her suffering from acute appendicitis and had her transferred immediately to Dudley Road hospital.

She remained with the force for 20 years. By 1939 she was found to be suffering from post-influenzal debility which made her 'incapacitated by infirmity of body' and the force doctor recommended her for medical retirement. She retired in March 1939 at the age of 72.

Ellen Vernon's uniform has been preserved and is held within the West Midlands Police Museum collection.

Hancox   Sarah Ann

Sarah Hancox was 49 and married when she joined Birmingham City Police in January 1919. She registered an interest in joining in December 1918 and when local officers carried out discreet enquiries into her character, it was reported that she was '48 years of age (but looks younger), was 5'4" in height, of good physique and very active (weight 10 stone)'.

It was reported she had served in the Women's Voluntary Reserve for the previous four years.

Similar to the other early women police, Mrs Hancox was made of tough stuff – in May 1935 whilst bending down to remove the shoes of a drunken female prisoner she was accidentally bumped in the side by the prisoner whereby she received a cracked rib. Bear in mind she was 66 years of age at this point! She did not wish to report sick and continued her duty, even though she was unable to take a deep breath without pain. Aside from having to have strapping to support the rib, she did not let this affect her police work.

She reported sick in May 1937 after suffering what appeared to be a heart attack and never returned to duty. The force doctor signed her off as medically unfit for further service as she was suffering from heart disease and she retired on a medical pension in June 1937, aged 68.

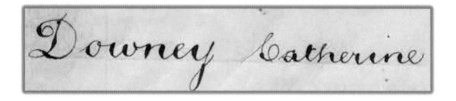

Although christened Catherine Downey, everybody in her family called her Kate. Born on February 9th 1871 in Kilglas, Ahascragh, County Galway, Eire, Kate was the fourth child in a family of eleven. Her parents were Andrew Downey and Anne Geraghty who married in

1867 in the village church in Ahascragh. Times were hard, money scarce and living conditions in the small farm cottage extremely cramped. They eked a living from the land.

In 1895, aged 24, Kate sailed from Cobh (or Queenstown, as it was then known) in County Cork, to New York on "The Germanic." She arrived in New York on July 25th 1895. The passenger records describe her occupation as a servant.

In the 1910 New York census she was 40 years old and living with John (32) and Helen Humber (35), proprietors of a saloon bar in Manhattan. Helen was Kate's younger sister. Also living at that address was James Downey (42) Kate's older brother, with whom she may have emigrated 15 years earlier.

Kate was working as a finisher in a knitting mill in New York and James was a carpenter. Whilst living and working in New York, Kate became engaged to a young man who was then killed in an accident there. Following this tragedy, Kate left New York and made her way to Birmingham.

She settled at 62 Stratford Road, Sparkhill, a mere 1.2 miles away from Sparkhill Police Station where the force museum was set up in 1995, and worked at the Women's Hospital as a nurse. Kate first inquired about joining the force as a policewoman In November 1918. On January 13th 1919, she joined the Birmingham City Police as one of the first 10 policewomen earning 35/- per week. Her height is recorded as 5'8", so she was one of the tallest early women police.

Kate was 48 years old when she joined in 1919 and, after completing 25 years' service, she retired on 19th March 1944, aged 73 years. Her record states she had 22 days of sick leave throughout her service. Her annual pay at the date of her leaving was £208.0.0 per annum and her pension was £104.0.0 per annum.

Initially, Kate lodged with a fellow colleague - Mrs Ellen Vernon, known as Sally. They lived in Alexandra Road, Handsworth in Sally Vernon's house.

Kate's great niece Eileen Robinson has provided a fascinating insight into her life, which she learned from her mother who was Kate's niece:

'In 1935, Kate returned to her home in County Galway for a holiday. She stayed at the family home which was then lived in by her younger brother, Andrew, his wife, Anne and children, Mary (my mother), Joseph and Robert. Poverty was commonplace at this time and rural Irish life presented few opportunities for the children. With this in mind, Kate decided to take Mary, who was 13 at the time, back to England with her.

They continued to lodge with Sally Vernon and I remember my mum telling me what a terrifying experience it was for her trying to adapt to all the changes that life in a big, noisy city required. Kate bought her a whole new wardrobe of clothes and shoes, had her hair cut and restyled and paid for a commercial education for her at Soho College in Soho Hill, Handsworth where she acquired full secretarial skills until she was 16. Mary's first post was as a shorthand typist at W. Canning Ltd in Constitution Hill.'

Kate and Ellen Vernon on patrol

In 1937, Kate had saved sufficient money to buy a house of her own. Some new houses had been constructed opposite Sally Vernon's house in Alexandra Road, Handsworth. Kate bought one of these and Kate and Mary moved in later that year. A few years later, Kate sent for Mary's younger brother, Joseph, doing exactly the same for him as she had done for Mary a few years earlier. A report in her file states she has accepted responsibility for her niece and nephew as their mother is 'delicate and not able to look after them'.

The outbreak of war saw 14 year old Joe evacuated to Monmouth with St Mary's RC School. Kate paid a visit to him there and was not happy with the situation. She felt he was lacking discipline, learning little and spending his life "playing games!" Later, she wrote to Joe telling him she wanted him home. This resulted in the headmaster Mr Tom O' Loughlin, writing a letter of complaint to the Chief Constable - he did not wish a 14 year old boy to travel unaccompanied, but meanwhile Kate was writing to him and telling him to ignore his teachers, pack up his things and leave with the train fare she had sent him! Kate was nevertheless determined to bring Joe home so she collected him herself and paid for him to attend a technical course at Greenmore College. He subsequently worked as an electrical engineer at the Austin Motor Company.

Eileen states 'Kate did all this for her niece and nephew whilst holding down a full time job throughout the War. Moreover, to buy a house as a single woman in these times when women were relatively disadvantaged showed such strength of character and determination. She gave two adolescents such a valuable start in life at her own expense and was an extremely committed and caring guardian to them both. They both finished up being very successful in their careers and both attribute this to the guidance and support given to them by Kate in their formative years. Life would undoubtedly have been very different for them without her intervention.'

Her cousins Detective Sergeant Andrew Downey and PC Michael Downey both also worked in the Birmingham force.

In 1944 she felt the need to resign as she had completed 25 years' service and was by this point 73 years of age. Until the research carried out for this book identified Evelyn Miles as being 77 when she retired, Kate was believed to have held the record for the oldest serving police woman.

Kate's niece got married and had two daughters before Kate became frail. They then moved in with Kate as a family to enable her niece to look after her. Kate died in 1952 aged 81 years.

In conclusion, Kate was a truly remarkable and inspirational woman – a woman ahead of her time.

The final woman who joined in January 1919 was Adelaide Pearce. She was born Adelaide Beresford in October 1884 and had three brothers.

She applied to join in August 1918 and stated she was 34 years of age and her husband was a soldier presently in France. She stated in her letter of interest to the Chief Constable that she was 'strong, well made and 5'9" tall'. Adelaide has several glowing references supporting her character in her file.

In 1940 she became a widow and in August 1942 she was medically retired, aged 57.

1917 to 1920: The Early Days

At this time the police headquarters was based at 55 Newton Street and this is where the Women Police worked from.

Many reports written by Sergeant Miles are held by the museum discussing the work of the Birmingham City Women's Police Department. These give valuable insight into not only the work of the officers but social problems and attitudes at the time. They also serve to demonstrate the increasing and ever changing work of the women in this department.

In an official report to Chief Constable Charles Haughton Rafter on February 21st 1920[55], Sergeant Miles summarises the work done by the department to date.

She writes that two former lock-up matrons joined on the 4th June 1917 and became the first women of the Women's Police Department. She is referring to herself and Mrs Lipscombe although their records state their official start date as 30th April. Their duties involved patrolling the streets and visiting public places such as libraries, coffee houses, lodging houses and railways. They found many young girls wondering the streets during the day and night, often visiting New Street Station and awaiting trains bringing soldiers. One of the officers started patrolling New Street Station at night but found it impossible to do the work alone.

During the first year of the department being in existence, they dealt with 91 girls with the following outcomes:

35	Taken to the night shelter
6	Roman Catholics – taken to Sister Catherine the Hostel
4	Taken to the Salvation Army
16	Sent home to parents or friends

30	Suffering from venereal disease – taken to Western Road House for treatment

Work and lodgings were found for many of these girls. After finding that most of them needed a place to stay while more permanent arrangements were made, in October 1917 the Chief Constable requested that the Judicial Sub-Committee approve finding a small house or that an arrangement be made with some reliable women for the lodging of unfortunate women until some satisfactory arrangement could be made for their disposal.[56]

By December a suitable house had still not been found and the Chief Constable reported that they had experienced considerable difficulty in obtaining the required accommodation, which needed to be close to the centre of the city and big enough for their purposes[57]. Mr Alderman Sayer informed the Judicial Sub-Committee that he would be prepared to offer the police force some premises belonging to him in Dale End, which the Chief Constable stated would be quite suitable for the required purpose.

Mr Alderman Sayer suggested that an agreed rent for these premises should be paid by the police and that it should be paid directly to the Police Aided Association for clothing the destitute children of Birmingham. This was an incredibly generous offer which was accepted by the committee and fit in well with the work of the women police as they spent considerable time and effort over the next few decades working with the Police Aided Association to help provide shoes, boots and clothes to families who were struggling.

Following inspection by the Chief Constable and the Women Police, some alterations to the premises were recommended to make it

suitable for the purposes of a lodging house for women brought in by the officers, the cost of this work being £290, which was approved by the Watch Committee in January 1918[58].

Alderman Sayer - Reproduced with the permission of the Library of Birmingham

The house at 67 Dale End, Birmingham was opened by the Watch Committee on the 7th June 1918. A Ladies Advisory Committee was appointed to oversee the work of this house[59]. The agreed rent ended up being a nominal fee of £50 per annum rent, which as promised Mr Alderman Sayer donated to the Police Aided Association[60]. The hostel was a success and is believed to have been the first of its kind in the country.

The officers found this greatly aided their work and allowed them to ensure the girls were in a place of safety whilst they made further enquiries or found them work or more permanent lodgings.

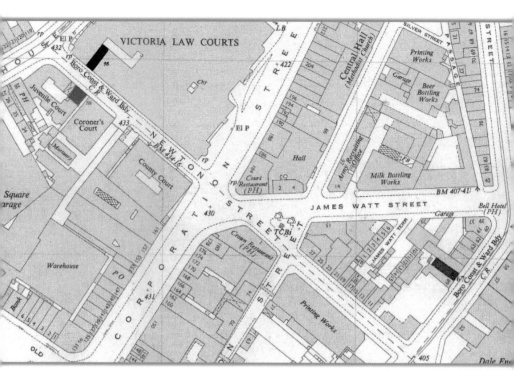

The above map demonstrates the proximity of the police HQ at 55 Newton Street (in blue) where the policewomen were originally based, 67 Dale End (in pink) where the first girls' hostel was located and 58 Newton Street (in red) where the second girls' hostel was later opened.

The Police Aided Association operated out of Digbeth Police Station. It was created in 1895 and is often referred to as the Police Aided Association for Clothing Destitute Children. It had branches around the country in most major cities. The Birmingham branch is recorded as helping an average of 62 cases per day in February 1895[61] and is frequently mentioned in Police Orders where assistance is requested.

One such time was recorded in October 1918[62] when members of the force were asked if they had a wife, sister or 'lady friend' who would be willing to help with street collections as they were very short of funds. The charity's aims were recorded as 'to provide footwear and clothing for poor children of the city, thereby alleviating distress'.[63]

Birmingham Police Aided Association post card, West Midlands Police Museum

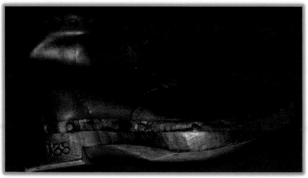

Police Aided Association shoe collection box, West Midlands Police Museum

In July 1918 Mrs Miles was complimented on services she had rendered in a letter received by the Watch Committee from the coroner of East Worcestershire. At the same meeting of the committee, it was approved that she be promoted to the rank of sergeant and her wages were increased to 50/- per week with a war bonus of 5/- per week.[64]

It was at this time that more women became involved with the girls hostel in Dale End – a Dr Lena Walker was recommended to become the visiting medical officer to the hostel and to be paid a rate of 10/6 per case and a Miss Knight to be co-opted as a member of the Ladies Advisory Committee[65]. The appointment of a female doctor demonstrates further the increase of females into traditional male roles during the early part of the 20th century.

A Miss Kate Lewis-Short has been referenced as the woman in charge of the Dale End house throughout the 1920s. Before being appointed to run the Dale End Hostel, Miss Short ran a hostel as a volunteer between 1906 and 1918. Watch Committee minutes from March 1926[66] show that the salary of Miss Short, matron of the girls' hostel Dale End, be increased as from 1st April 1926 from £100 to £120 per annum, with board and lodgings.

Police Orders from October 1918[67] show that a £10.10.0 contribution was to be paid to the funds of the Girls' Night Shelter in Tenant Street on behalf of the Committee, in accordance with the usual practice. This demonstrates the financial commitment from the police to supporting women's shelters to help women in need, in addition to running their own hostel.

The workload rapidly increased and the social work element of the work of the female police became clearer. Over the following 18 months until 31st December 1919, 190 cases were dealt with and a wider variety of outcomes achieved than the first 12 months (note some cases have more than one outcome recorded):

37	Girls taken home to parents or relatives
34	To training homes
26	Into domestic service
48	Employment found in factories and lodgings found
6	Maternity cases
4	Mothers with young babies taken to the workhouse
9	Certified mentally deficient
14	To Sister Catherine Hostel (Roman Catholic)
12	Lost sight of
46	Girls taken to the infirmary suffering from venereal disease
18	Others found in a dirty and verminous condition and removed to Western Road House for Treatment

In 1919 Sergeant Miles applied to the Chief Constable to petition the Watch Committee for more pay. She stated it had been 16 months since she was appointed and the work had not only increased considerably but become much more arduous. She refers to the high cost of living and house rent. This petition appears to be successful as at the start of 1920 her pay increased to 72/- per week.

A report from Miss Short at the women's hostel in Dale End to the Judicial Sub-Committee in October 1919 stated that 72 cases had been admitted to the home during the previous six months and the result was entirely satisfactory.[68]

A high number of girls and women were found to be suffering from venereal disease. This had been a social problem in the UK since the 1800s and Parliament first passed legislation to try to deal with it in 1864, with amendments being made in 1866 and 1869. The Contagious

Diseases Acts gave police officers the power to detain women suspected of being a prostitute for a period of three months whilst they were treated for the disease. Note that nothing whatsoever was done about the men who were likely also to be carrying and spreading the disease. Initially the Acts only applied to naval ports and army towns but was extended to cover further districts. The length of time a women could be detained also increased up to a period of one year. After much campaigning against the unfair treatment of any women 'suspected to be' a prostitute, the incredibly painful examination procedures many women had been subject to and the clear inequalities between men and women demonstrated by the legislation, in 1886 the Acts were finally repealed[69]. The Venereal Disease Act 1917 had provisions to ensure treatment was only given by medically qualified practitioners. Police Orders in 1918 refer to the 'evils resulting from the treatment of venereal disease by unqualified practitioners'.[70]

As evidenced by the reports of the Women Police Department in Birmingham throughout the 1920s and 1930s, venereal disease was still a major social issue.

Training homes were similar to workhouses but taught specific skills. Children were taught skills such as spinning and weaving and any income generated from their work often went to the running of the school.

The report for 1919 talks about complaints being received about girls visiting the Chinese lodgings and a number of girls aged 16-19 being found at 'these houses'. Raids were carried out at night with plain clothes officers and any girls found were taken to the Dale End house. A summary of this work indicates 12 girls had married Chinese men and given birth to children and 'many others have unfortunately become pregnant'. No indication was given of any criminality being undertaken by the Chinese men, indeed it doesn't state that any of them were arrested, so one must conclude that the problem seen at the time was the sexual activity of young women (although not always outside of marriage) and the fact that lots of this activity was centred around the Chinese lodgings. Whilst not explicitly stated, were the inter-race relationships also considered a problem needing to be addressed?

Sergeant Miles goes on to talk about prostitution (or 'leading an immoral life' as she referred to it) and states over 25% of these girls were under 17 years of age.

The officers found many girls in dire need of clothing and food and would often supply clothing and boots for them. A great many 'friends of the department' who were interested in the work of the women police donated clothing and boots.

The officers regularly found the wives and children of army deserters living in extreme poverty. They would give immediate assistance where possible and notify parish authorities.

One of the last paragraphs of this first report is a very clear indication of how times have changed over the past 100 years:

'We also had brought to our notice two cases of women cohabiting with men, and having large families by them. These women we persuaded to go into the workhouse for the sake of the children.'

A plaque placed at the original entrance to the old Birmingham Workhouse and unveiled by Professor Carl Chinn in 1999 stated it was known locally as the 'Arch of Tears' – giving an insight into how it was perceived and the distress of many of the former residents. The plaque states 'In life they endured misfortune – in death they may rest in peace'[71]. This shows just how much social attitudes have evolved, that for unmarried mothers to go into the workhouse and be separated from their children, was better than to remain cohabiting with the children and their father.

Based on the fact that Sergeant Miles herself was unmarried with a baby at 18 years of age, perhaps her reasoning for asking the women to go into the workhouse focussed on ensuring the children were fed and clothed, and not so much on the scandal that having children outside of wedlock would have caused back in the early 1900s. After all her experience of the previous few years would have exposed her to many cases of families living in extreme poverty without sufficient clothing or food for the children.

The final statement by Sergeant Miles in this report indicates they like to follow up on all cases and that many of the girls are now doing well.

Lady Enquiry Officers

Lady enquiry officer is also referred to as female enquiry officer and is a role that first appeared in 1919 in the Birmingham City Police.

Records show that a Miss Emily Mary Wayland was recruited as the first lady enquiry officer within the Birmingham City Police's Criminal Investigation Department. She was appointed on the 24th November 1919 and commenced her work at a salary of £3 per week, 1/6 per week boot allowance and £14 per annum in lieu of a uniform. Her record shows that she was 41 when she joined. She did not stay very long – it was reported to the Judicial Sub-Committee in October 1920 that she had resigned following her refusal to adopt certain procedures of the department and she left on the 30th October 1920.[72] A letter in Miss Dorothy Peto's file indicates Miss Wayland declined to go through a course at the police school, which was a requirement of all the Women Police.[73]

Miss Dorothy Peto replaced her and remained with the force for four years. She left and went on to become the highest ranking female officer within the Metropolitan Police before her retirement.

She was followed by a Miss Mildred White in 1925 who went on to continue her successful policing career, having been one of the first attested female officers in the UK, in Salisbury in 1915.

A few months after Miss White was promoted to inspector, a Miss Joan Alexander was appointed at the rank of sergeant, also as a lady enquiry officer. She remained with the force for three years.

The work carried out by the lady enquiry officer consisted mainly of investigation of crimes relating to women and children, particularly sexual offences, use of indecent language and abortion.

Dorothy Olivia Georgiana Peto got involved with the Voluntary Women Patrols when she enrolled in the city of Bath in 1914. She became the director of the Bristol Training School for Women Police in 1917. This school was responsible for training potential female police officers, munitions police, voluntary patrols, the Women's Royal Air Force and the Queen Mary's Army Auxiliary Corps. She was involved in advocating the need for women police from the very early days and her varied career within the police and different social organisations included a four-year stint with Birmingham City Police from 1920 to 1924. She eventually became the superintendent in charge of the

Women's Police Department in the Metropolitan Police Service (equivalent to a chief superintendent in today's structure).

When the Bristol Training School shut down after the Baird Committee had concluded, Miss Peto set about applying to different forces for an appointment at a rank not below inspector, and unsurprisingly with no actual experience within a police force, was finding it difficult to obtain one! Notwithstanding the fact that at this time it would have been highly unlikely for any police force to have a female officer above the rank of sergeant. When discussing the matter with her friend, Sir Leonard Dunning, he told her to apply for a position, not mention rank, and see what came of it – which she did[74].

Miss Peto applied for a position with the Birmingham Police's Criminal Investigation Department (CID) in 1920 and she was successfully appointed to the role of lady enquiry officer. She was told straight away that this was separate to Sergeant Miles' uniformed Women Police Department.

Dorothy Peto, Metropolitan Police, courtesy of the Met Heritage Centre

The Watch Committee minutes from November 1920 show Miss D.O.G. Peto was appointed as female enquiry officer in the Criminal Investigation Department at a salary of £200, with £14 plain clothes allowance and 2/- per week boot allowance in lieu of a uniform[75]. Excluding the allowances for boots and clothing, this amounts to 26/- a week more than a policewoman's starting salary of 50/- a week in 1922 and still a further 11/- on what a policewoman could be earning after nine years' service.

She states in her memoirs she instantly disliked her title and promptly replaced the word lady with detective, soon becoming known as the detective enquiry officer! [76]

Miss Peto attended a normal probationer's course and CID training, whilst being on call day and night to take statements in relation to sexual offences and to be on hand for examinations of victims of sexual assaults.

She talks about being accompanied by a detective inspector on any visits to victims or witnesses for statements and being prompted on all questions to be asked. She also recalls her first occasion of being unaccompanied – when the smell of the house they attended was so great her male companion had to wait outside and left her to it!

Miss Peto spoke of 'Sergeant Mrs Miles' very fondly and stated 'a better friend and colleague one could not have had the good fortune to find'. She also spoke highly of Chief Superintendent Burnett who was head of the CID during her time in Birmingham and responsible for introducing lady enquiry officers to the force.

James Taylor Burnett was born on 7th December 1870 and joined the Birmingham City Police on the 10th January 1893. He was promoted to superintendent on 3rd July 1916 and on 2nd October 1918 he was appointed to take charge of the Criminal Investigation Department, later being promoted to chief superintendent in the same department. He was complimented by the Home Secretary in 1918 for work done in connection with numerous enquiries and reports as to aliens and suspected persons which have been of great assistance in carrying out the duties of the war office and on 1st January 1920 he was awarded the MBE for special services rendered during the war.

Chief Superintendent James Taylor Burnett

His service continued until March 1935 when he died in the Dingle Nursing Home, aged 64. He had been suffering from pleurisy and pneumonia since February 1935.

She stated he 'was a large, impassive Scot, a man of few words' who accepted only the best from his officers. One story is recalled from the time of the onset of the Great Depression, whereby a party of unemployed men from the North were on route to London on foot to join a demonstration. When they reached Birmingham, Chief Superintendent Burnett dealt with them personally. He was said to have talked with them very wisely in a fatherly manner, made sure they had food and shelter for the night and convinced them to accept fares for the train home the next day. Miss Peto stated she had no idea where he got the money from, and it is likely he paid for the fares out of his own pocket.

Miss Peto talks of how different the Birmingham folk were from the easy going people of Bristol. She states how accommodating they were to female officers and how on many occasions the relief of victims, witnesses and their mothers was obvious when they saw a female police officer had come to receive their statement.

Her recollections also highlight how different medical examinations were to the procedures utilised nowadays. On most occasions it was carried out by the police surgeon in the matron's office at the local station and put the victim through quite an ordeal – often unnecessarily because the officer in charge thought it best to be on the safe side. She does however recall one particular surgeon – Dr. MacCready – who did his very best to make the procedure as harmless as possible. He would invite the victim and their mother to his surgery and make it seem as much like a normal check-up as possible – often by engaging in games with the child whilst he quickly checked to identify if an assault had taken place.

Another shocking difference between modern practices and those from the early days of the women police was identity parades. Miss Peto refers to the victim having to physically walk past the suspect and the stooges (often recruited from the local labour exchange and made up to look as much like the suspect as possible with various accessories) and actually touch the person they believe to be the offender. A standing order was issued in 1924 that officers involved in the investigation must not be present during the identity parade. This would help to eliminate allegations of foul play but must have made it all the more difficult for the victim, who might then have to go through the terrifying procedure without anyone familiar to them.

A further insight into the work of female officers at this time period is given when she talks about any spare time leading to work tracing the families of servicemen killed during the First World War in order to hand over medals or to establish details of dependants entitled to a war pension. It would appear there was a large supply of this work needing to be done. Note that this work was specifically for the lady enquiry officer in the CID, not the uniformed women's police.

In 1922 she was authorised to routinely enter premises for the purpose of inspecting registers for domestic servants.[77]

In 1923 the Home Secretary announced the Metropolitan Women Police were to be sworn in as constables. This news arrived in Birmingham and Miss Peto recalls being out on the trail of a man suspected of a number of indecent assaults, when the inspector she was with spotted the suspect and said to her 'go on Miss Peto, women are constables now! You go over and make the arrest'. Not one to miss out on the opportunity of actually making an arrest she decided not to inform him that it didn't actually apply to their own force and her common law powers of arrest in such matters did not come into force until after 9:00pm, instead marching straight over and making the arrest. Needless to say the arrest was attributed to the inspector on the charge sheet.

In 1924 Miss Peto left Birmingham as her father had died and she needed to find work closer to home. Her pension contributions of £20.2.3 were returned to her[78] and the Chief Constable later provided a certificate of service for her and stated Birmingham City Police were 'free from pension liability in this case'.[79]

She was pleased to see appointed in her place a Sergeant White who was an attested officer from Salisbury Police and was successful in requesting that she be sworn in upon arrival in Birmingham and be able to transfer her rank. Sergeant Miles and the rest of her uniform branch were not attested until October 1931.

Dorothy Peto went on to become the first female superintendent at the Metropolitan Police and was appointed an Officer of the Order of the British Empire in 1920 and awarded the King's Police and Fire Services Medal in 1944.

Dorothy Peto, left, after her retirement from the police service

The 'Roaring 20s' – Onwards and Upwards

At the beginning of the 1920s, partner agencies started to engage more with the women police. In March 1920 the Maternity Hospital asked for an officer to be on hand every time an ambulance case was transferred to the hospital. This was denied, due to the impracticable aspect of the request – that you would need an officer permanently based there in order to respond to the unpredictable nature of the work.[80]

At this point the work of the female watchers (who were required to keep watch over female prisoners who had attempted suicide) was scaled back and limited only to 'special cases', for which their remuneration would be increased to 5/- a day.[81] The Watch Committee requested that the Chief Constable update local hospitals to this effect.

At the Judicial Sub-Committee on 28th January 1921 the Chief Constable submitted a return asked for by the Salaries, Wages &

Labour Committee with reference to married woman employed in the police force.

This relates to a letter received by the Salaries, Wages and Labour Committee on 23rd December 1920 from the National Alliance of Employers and Employed, which stated the following[82]:

Dear Sir,

Unemployment

The question of unemployment in Birmingham and the District was discussed at a meeting of the Birmingham and the District Committee of the National Alliance of Employers and Employed on Tuesday last, 23rd inst. The Committee noted with satisfaction the steps that are being taken by the Lord Mayor in conjunction with the Unemployment Committee, and are ~~very~~ anxious to co-operate in every way possible, to alleviate unemployment in this district.

I have been instructed to forward a copy of the resolution given below to all members - Employers, Associations and Trade Unions - affiliated to the Local Council of the Alliance, asking them to consider this resolution and to put same into operation, where practicable:-

'That this Committee is of the opinion that distinct hardship, to some of the unemployed, is caused by the fact that Married Women are being retained in employment, while their husbands are in receipt of wages, and we strongly urge, where possible, that un-Married Women or Men should be employed.'

Some time ago our National Executive Committee

viewing with apprehension the increasing rate of unemployment throughout the country, set up a sub-Committee to consider ways and means of alleviating, and if possible mitigating same. A Deputation from the Alliance was received by the Minister of Labour of Tuesday 7th December, and put forward certain proposals. A brief report of this interview is attached, together with a copy of the four resolutions, which were forwarded to the Prime Minister and the Minister of Labour, prior to the Deputation being received.

Yours faithfully, A.H. Ryman
Hon Sec. pro tem.

It was resolved at the Judicial Sub-Committee that 'the clerk be instructed to forward the return to the Salaries, Wages & Labour Committee, at the same time pointing out that the business of the Police Department necessitated great care in the selection of women employed, together with special training, and whilst the Committee were in sympathy with the resolution contained in the letter from Salaries Wages & Labour Committee they regretted the circumstances they had indicated would in their opinion prevent its application in the Police Department'[83]. This demonstrates the police service starting to break away from sexist practises and move towards equality.

By the end of 1921 the workload had increased considerably – with a total of 1,137 women and girls being dealt with. 121 were taken to the police hostel in Dale End with the following outcomes:

29	Have been taken or sent to their friends
27	Have been sent to training homes
23	Into domestic service
3	Employment found in factories
4	Certified mentally deficient
9	Pregnant – taken to Hope Lodge or workhouse maternity wards

12	Suffering from venereal disease, taken for treatment to Western Road House
10	Mothers & babies kept until suitable home found for them
4	Lost sight of

A further 80 girls passed through the home, often staying only one night and many of these were brought in by male officers.

The remaining 1016 women and girls were dealt with from Newton Street Police Station as follows:

155	Employment found in factories or domestic service
64	Were found lodgings
20	Found stranded and taken back to friends
14	Taken to workhouse (verminous)
53	Taken to hospital
42	To Flight Shelter, Felix House (Dale End being full)
24	To Bath Street Hostel (Roman Catholic)
11	To St. Mary's Hostel (Y.W.C.A) St. Mary's Row
7	To Shaftsbury House
4	Certified mentally deficient
36	Pregnant, taken to Hope Lodge or maternity wards
25	Venereal cases, taken to Western Road House
87	Destitute – taken to the workhouse
227	Given food, clothing and advice.
196	Visits paid by request of parents regarding daughters and young girls found continually on the streets
49	Visits paid to settle differences between husbands and wives etc

Shaftsbury House is recorded as a Working Girl's Hostel on the same road as the Y.W.C.A. at St. Mary's Hostel on St. Mary's Row.

Western Road House was the infirmary attached to the workhouse but you did not have to be a resident of the workhouse to use it.

These figures show that 32% of cases dealt with by the Women Police had a social care outcome and led to the women being taken care of by one institution of another, including the workhouse, hospitals and hostels. 9% were taken to the workhouse and this rises to 12% when including those who went to the workhouse infirmary for treatment for venereal disease. Children were often sent to the workhouse when their mothers were sent to prison.

An important development for the women police in Birmingham occurred in January 1922: at the Judicial Sub-Committee the recommendation was made to the Watch Committee for the women to be made permanent[84]. This demonstrates the original intention to employ women police officers on a 'trial basis' which had clearly been a success. It was also stated that the women would qualify for superannuation and be allowed to count the whole of their service since their date of appointment, provided they pay arrears in superannuation deductions, as laid out by the Chief Constable.

The work in 1922 included additional duties such as attending Assizes, Sessions and Children's Courts as matrons, relief matrons and court matron. They were responsible for escorting convicted women, taking young girls and boys to and from remand homes or workhouses and taking girls home to their parents. Sergeant Miles also highlights how the female officers dealt with complaints from husbands and wives and often helped to bring couples back together who may have been apart for a considerable length of time.

The number of cases of unmarried mothers and expectant mothers was reported as being 'very, very great during the past five years' and was clearly a concern for the Women Police. Even though the mothers were often not able to keep their children with them, the police were a vital support network for these women who were often shunned by their families and society. In most cases work was found for the mother and a foster family for the child. Chinese men living in rented accommodation were stated as being responsible for many of the children born to these girls.

Numerous girls were found sleeping rough and described as being in a 'dirty and verminous condition, and taken to the workhouse to be cleansed'. What became of them after this is not recorded.

During the early part of 1923, Councillor Miss Wilson was appointed to the Ladies Advisory Committee who oversaw the running of the Dale End hostel for girls.

In January 1923 the Chief Constable was considering replacing the Dale End hostel and asked the city surveyor to consider whether alterations could be made to 54 and 56 Newton Street so that these buildings could be re-purposed for use as a girls' hostel[85] (bearing in mind the police headquarters were based at 55 Newton Street at this time). It was requested that Miss Wilson provide a report on the suitability of the Dale End premises.

In February 1923 Councillor Miss Wilson reported that as requested by the sub–committee that she had visited the hostel and discussed the question of accommodation with Mrs. Osler, the Chairman of the Ladies Advisory Committee, with the result that she had formed the conclusion that the house was a very inconvenient one and did not lend itself to proper supervision, and that proper accommodation was needed if the work was to be carried on satisfactorily in the future[86].

Councillor Miss Wilson was thanked for her services and it was requested that she be asked to interview the city surveyor and inform him of the requirements needed in order to provide for the amenities of the home.

In March 1923 a letter was read to the Judicial Sub-Committee from Mrs Osler stating that the committee had been through the City Surveyor's plans for the Newton Street building and they could not see a reasonable way of making the house suitable for their purposes[87]. Miss Wilson requested that the Ladies Advisory Committee be authorised to employ an agent to keep a look-out for suitable alternative premises and this was approved.

By the end of 1923 the caseload had gone up to 1,349 with similar outcomes being obtained.

Of note:

- 60 were given food and lodgings – many of these were strangers to Birmingham, which was becoming an increasingly desirable location for those seeking a better quality of life.
- 50 were taken to court and summonses obtained for 'desertion, affiliation, assault etc'.

The department was still providing temporary and relief matrons for the lock-up and it was highlighted that work was found for many women and girls who were discharged prisoners and had been sent to them by the Chaplain or 'Lady Visitors of the prison'. The workload was described as 'strenuous' for the department which, according to Sergeant Miles' reports, at this time only consisted of six women and their sergeant. Lizzie May Peers, Mary Dwelly and Malenda Shaw had left by now, therefore Elsie Chapman – court matron and part time policewoman – was being included in the numbers for the department.

The report for 1924 is the first time the workload is noted as including taking statements for sexual offences – 260 statements are recorded for offences including incest, rape, indecent assault and indecent exposures or suggestions. Since the lady enquiry officer post was created in CID in 1919, this individual would have carried out this work alone. There is a gap of seven months between Dorothy Peto leaving and Florence White starting, presumably the Women Police filled this gap.

Sergeant Miles records a significant issue of middle aged women being supported in finding work and the difficulty in obtaining lodgings for them. She writes 'May I say that it is one of our City's greatest needs, a common lodging house for women'. This alludes to a wider social housing crisis being experienced in Birmingham at the time.

In December 1924 the treasurer for the Girls' Night Shelter (separate to the police run girls' hostel) made a request for funds from the Judicial Sub-Committee. The matter was discussed and it was determined that on the basis of the usefulness of the shelter to the police, a request would be made to the Finance Committee for them to make a subscription of £10.10.0 in their next allotment of contributions to hospitals and other charitable organisations.[88] This appears to be a shelter supported by frequent donations from the Birmingham City Police.

1924 was the year of the next Home Office committee looking into the role of women police - the Bridgeman Committee. Sir Charles Haughton Rafter was one of the Chief Constables in attendance who came out in support of women police. He was able to highlight the valuable work carried out by Sergeant Miles and her team. The recommendations of the Bridgeman Committee were largely supportive of women police, but the Home Office still left their employment up to the local discretion of police forces.

In 1926 it is recorded that half of the women and girls taken to the Dale End house had been leading 'an immoral life'. This could have been through prostitution, girls associating with men outside of marriage or women finding themselves pregnant outside of wedlock.

In 1928 a Royal Commission on Police Powers and Procedures was appointed and again the role of women police was considered. Charles Haughton Rafter was once more asked to give evidence and he stated his officers had been a success and he would like further women police.[89]

By the start of 1929 the yearly caseload was 2,674. By now Sergeant Miles indicates 75% of girls leading an 'immoral life' were under 18 years of age. The percentage of girls and women being sent to various institutions was now 10% with many more being found work, lodgings or simply given advice. This is not necessarily an indication of the decline of institutional care being provided as the numbers are still high – but more likely an indication that more individuals were coming to the Women Police for clothing, food or advice and there was also an increase in the number of referrals from concerned parents or friends. These reasons cater for 77% of cases.

The issue of unmarried mothers and expectant mothers was reported as increasing. Many of the women were described as 'very respectable' and their condition traced back to going on motor or motorcycle rides into the country with men who gave them false details.

2,975 cases were recorded for 1929 and a police hostel was now being utilised at 58 Newton Street, opposite the police headquarters. This hostel was opened in 1928 when the premises at 67 Dale End were outgrown and transferred to Newton Street. These premises were donated by the Barrow Cadbury family[90]. Watch Committee minutes from 5th June 1929[91] show that 'girls from 10 years of age and upwards awaiting trial or on remand or awaiting transference to Home Office schools shall be received at the girls' hostel, Newton Street'. The city surveyor was to be instructed to make the necessary alterations to 'provide for the separation of different classes of persons to be maintained in these homes'.

Miss Short is still employed to oversee the running of the hostel and she is recorded here as advising on girls being sent to training homes from the police hostel at Newton Street.

In October 1929 the requirements for the Women Police are included on the force's list of uniform items to be purchased, namely[92]:

- Mackintoshes @ 34/9
- Blouses @ 10/6
- Collars @ 8 ½d
- Ties @1/4
- Tunics and skirts (winter weight) @ £7.10.0

In 1929 the Royal Commission on Police Powers and Procedure praised the Birmingham City Police force for pioneering the appointment of women police constables. In his evidence to the commission, Chief Constable Sir Charles Haughton Rafter had outlined the preventative work that his women police had been undertaking[93] and also stated that they protected male officers from the sort of complaints "readily and glibly made" by "the class of women who usually come into Police custody"[94].

The files held by the museum do not include all former Birmingham City officers, although the majority of early female officers' files are held. It should be noted that right up to the 1950s almost all officers are recorded and it is likely their files are held. From the 1950s onwards, certain records are held by the museum for officers who did not complete 30 years' service, but generally the files for officers who left during the 1960s and onwards are still held corporately by the force and are not available to the museum. Therefore all the statistics and generalisations made from the museum files come with the caveat that some individuals may be excluded. It should also be noted that the way the female files have been recorded, if an officer joined, left and re-joined – their information is recorded under the latter date and will be included in the statistics for that time period.

The files that are held give a very interesting insight into the make-up of these officers, where they had come from, their ages, marital status and when and why they left.

Of the fifteen officers who joined prior to 1930 whose records are held by the museum, four of these originated from outside of Birmingham, the locations being Bristol, Norfolk, Salisbury and as far away as South Africa! For the eight who have previous occupations recorded, these are all to do with the police/prison service (with the exception of one who was a hospital sister) - one even being a police officer from the Salisbury force (this was Florence White, Dorothy Peto's replacement). Just under half of the women (seven) were married.

From these officers we have the first sergeant in Birmingham (Evelyn Miles - 1918) and the first inspectors (Susan Palmer and Florence White - 1930).

Eight of the first fifteen officers left on superannuation after being granted a pension. Five of these were ill-health pensions with 10 achieving long policing careers and the remaining five leaving during their first five years.

Miss White joined Birmingham City Police in June 1925 and took over the role Dorothy Peto had been carrying out in the force's CID as lady enquiry officer. Although official documentation shows her as Florence Mildred White, she appeared to go by Mildred, and that is what she has signed on official correspondence.[95]

Miss White was born on the 10th December 1873 in Wiltshire and became one of the first attested policewomen in the country when she joined Salisbury Police in 1918. She was originally a language teacher working out of the prestigious Godolphin School in Salisbury, Wiltshire. She went on to join Salisbury Police in 1918 and remained there until the end of May 1925 when she transferred to Birmingham City Police.

In reply to Miss White's letter of interest in a vacancy in the Birmingham City Police, Chief Constable Charles Haughton Rafter stated 'Your hours of duty would be intermittent, that is, you would be called upon whenever cases arise for you to deal with.'[96] Whilst this sounds like an early example of a 'zero hours' contract, she was actually pretty busy most of the time and worked a full time job! A record of cases she dealt with in 1929 shows:

- Indecent language   9
- Indecent Exposure   226
- Common Assault   28
- Indecent Assault   125

- Carnal Knowledge of a girl between 13 and 16   12
- Carnal Knowledge of an Imbecile   2
- Incest and alleged Incest   4
- Abortion   1
- Alleged Rape   8

The language alone demonstrates a stark difference between policing in the 1920s and today – with rape only being recognised as 'alleged', to have 'carnal knowledge' of a girl and the word imbecile with reference to limited mental capacity.

When she transferred to Birmingham, Miss White requested to keep her sergeant rank and her powers of arrest. This was agreed and she was re-attested upon arrival in Birmingham – making her the first attested policewoman in the West Midlands.

Back in 1925 the Chief Constable of Salisbury Police Mr Frank Richardson had the good sense to acknowledge Miss White's eventual need for a pension – writing to Sir Charles Haughton Rafter upon her transfer to Birmingham and stating her time in Salisbury should count as 'approved service' and was therefore pensionable. He also cleared the matter with his own Watch Committee when she started there, ensuring she was superannuated.

In February 1937 she requested permission from her superintendent to resign. The Chief Constable wrote to the Home Office for advice as this was the first time a female officer in Birmingham had applied to resign on pension, with the particular issue that she had not completed the minimum length of service (25 years), or attained the compulsory retirement age or provided evidence to obtain a medical pension. We know from the Watch Committee minutes of 1922 that women could now qualify for a pension, however the issues stated above made this a bit more complex.

She was 63 years of age and would complete 19 years approved service by May 1937. The reply from the Home Office stated the position was 'rather awkward' – with Miss White's service having started in 1918 (before the 1921 Pension Act) so the provisions of that Act did not apply to her and as she had not completed 25 years' service nor did she have a medical certificate stating she could no longer work, she was actually not entitled to a pension at all. In a wonderful letter where Miss White articulately sums up her position and refers to the 1921 Pension Act, she stated:

'During the Great War, there was an urgent call for women to join the police service. Women responded to that call and, rather recklessly, did not wait for the passing of an act granting pensions to Policewomen.

I submit that women who joined in middle life did so with little hope of being able to serve efficiently for 25 years and that possibly a few others besides myself welcomed Section 2 (2) as providing a merciful 'avenue of escape'.

I cannot believe that those who framed the provisions of this Act ever intended that women should be allowed to continue in the service after the age of 60, (or 'in special cases' the age of 65).

It will be seen that I have now worked for some 44 years and I should now be very thankful to know I have earned my rest.[97]

The Home Office did not object to the Birmingham Watch Committee having the final say on the matter and with the Salisbury Police Authority agreeing to be liable for their proportion, Miss Florence White was finally able to retire aged 64 on the 31st May 1937.

Walsall officers

As documented earlier, Walsall women police were first recruited in 1918. They were followed by Alice Holland in April 1919 and Winifred Maud McLintic, who joined in December 1921.

Alice was born in 1879 in Birmingham and had previously been a nurse in a hospital. Both women had worked as munitions police officers in Gretna during the war. Alice began work there in May 1917 and remained until February 1919. She was single when she joined Walsall Borough Police and she stayed with the force until January 1925 when she went off sick with a breakdown. She never returned to work as she died in February 1925.

Winifred worked as a munitions police officer in Gretna from June 1918 to September 1919. A former dressmaker, she was born in Malta in 1891 and was also single when she joined. She later married and became Winifred Crooks whilst still with the force. She left in January 1931 at her own request.

It is likely that Walsall remained with only two policewomen posts for some time as additional recruits only arrived after other officers left – Marion Gray Ritchie (who only stayed with the force for one year) in

1925 to replace Alice Holland and two additional officers to fill Winifred and Marion's vacant posts in 1931.

According to the personnel ledgers, Walsall only ever recruited one married female officer and this wasn't until 1961. The only officer before then who wasn't single was a widow in 1952.

The women came from all over the United Kingdom – with some from Scotland, Liverpool, Durham, Pembrokeshire, Dorset, Essex and Kent.

Eight of the women had been police cadets. Many had clerical roles with seven having already worked as policewomen, two as prison officers and one as a member of the Women's Auxiliary Police Corps.

The reasons for leaving that are shown are broken down as follows:

- Four dismissed
- One left on medical grounds
- 37 left at their own request
- One was required to resign
- Five transferred out

Unfortunately several of the ledger entries are incomplete and we cannot see the dates the officers left or their reason for leaving. We can identify however that the shortest service was one day for an officer who joined in 1952!

The 1930s and the Run Up to War

By September 1930 a superintendent of the girls' hostel in Newton Street (Miss Rachel MacDonald Arnott) was appointed. In April 1931 it is stated she was discharging her duties satisfactorily and asked for her position to be made permanent. The Watch Committee was recommended to approve the appointment and the city treasurer was asked to arrange for Miss Arnott to enter into the superannuation scheme from her original start date.[98]

The Girls' Night Shelter was still being supported with a record in the Watch Committee minutes for 1930 showing that 10 guineas had been approved to be donated by the Chief Constable[99].

In 1930 the Watch Committee approved new pay, allowances and conditions of service for the female officers. Women Police Orders from 29th October 1930[100] show the newly approved pay scales for women police:

- Constable: £130 on appointment, up to a maximum of £195 after 20 or 22 years
- Sergeant: £234 on appointment, up to a maximum of £260 after four years
- Inspector: £260 on appointment, up to a maximum of £300 after four years

This was a reduction in salaries for many of the women – approximately 5/- less a week which left them in arrears for the month of October as the new scales were implemented from the 1st of the month.[101]

This compared to a male constable's starting salary in the same time period of approximately £182 (70/- per week).

In December 1930 the Chief Constable was authorised to purchase six 'great coats' for use of the Women Police at a cost of £5.15.0 each.[102]

Miss Short, the woman originally in charge of the girls' hostel in Dale End, retired in December 1930. The Watch Committee thanked her for 25 years' service on behalf of the women and girls of Birmingham. The Watch Committee wanted their sincere appreciation of her devoted work recorded, which they felt was deserving of the respect and gratitude of the citizens of Birmingham. It is recorded that 'the operation of the superannuation scheme has made it necessary for Miss Short to retire' and the committee regretted this. They were very grateful however that she offered to continue running the Newton Street Hostel until a replacement could be found. She was paid a £25 gratuity for this.[103]

By January 1931 the role of the Women Police was further expanding with 4,058 cases recorded. Nearly 10% are still sent or taken to various institutions including the workhouse and various children's homes. Almost half of the cases were visitors to Newton Street station for advice.

Sergeant Miles remarks on the ever increasing number of husbands and wives having trouble, but is pleased to report that in many cases the officers have helped to bring the couple back together. Another increasing problem was unmarried pregnant girls which had increased 100% on the previous year. Often these girls are recorded as being from respectable families and holding good positions working in the city. It is also noted that many were under 18 years of age and suffering from venereal disease.

The department still only consisted of six officers and with regular services being provided as court matron and relief matron at the lock-up, the depleted workforce certainly had their work cut out.

In April 1931 the Chief Constable reported that he had engaged five additional women police but that their premises were in a bad state of repair. The city surveyor was authorised to arrange for any necessary repairs and re-decoration of the women's quarters was to be undertaken[104].

In October 1931 a letter from the Home Office was received together with new Police (Women) Regulations by the Judicial Sub-Committee. Councillor Miss Wilson compared the new conditions to those already in force in Birmingham, particularly to the appointment of married women and rent allowances. It was resolved that the regulations be adopted and that the Chief Constable arrange for the women now serving in the force to be attested forthwith.

It was also requested that the Chief Constable communicate with the Home Office, putting forward the desirability of retaining the option of appointing married women to the police force.[105]

Police Orders for 14th October 1931[106] state:

'Police (Women) Regulations.

The Watch Committee having received from the Home Secretary Regulations concerning the appointment, discipline, pay etc., have adopted these Regulations, and in accordance with them all members of the Women Police Force will be forthwith attested, and arrangements should be made for this to be done at the Victoria Courts at 10 a.m. on Thursday 15th October.'

It goes on to note that supplementary deductions will be made from the inspectors and sergeants of the Women Police at the rate of 5% from the 5th October 1931.

Part of the new regulations stipulated that only unmarried or widowed women between the ages of 22 and 35 could be employed as women police officers. Interestingly no provisions were made in the regulations specifically for divorced women – only single or widowed.

From October through to December 1931, the Chief Constable was corresponding with the Home Office regarding the issue of married women police officers. The 1931 regulations did not allow women police officers to be married, but the majority of the Birmingham City women police were already married.

Married officers at the time were allowed to remain but a marriage ban was now instigated across all police forces (some already had them in place) so any serving officer who wanted to get married had to resign and new officers could not be married.

The minutes show the Chief Constable was requested to arrange for a modification of the conditions of service to meet the new circumstances.[107] A letter held in the file of one of the first female police officers Mrs Adelaide Pearce provides valuable information on how the issue of married female officers was addressed:

'In October 1931 on receipt of the new Police (Women) Regulations all the Women Police in Birmingham were attested; but as there were a number of married women then serving, the Chief Constable reported the matter to the Home Office. Mr Dixon replied on 26th October 1931, that the existing married women could be retained as police women, but their attestation was invalid, and they must remain unattested. The women concerned were advised to this effect.'

It can be seen in the married officers' files that they were attested in October 1931 and then it is crossed through with red pen with the word 'cancelled':

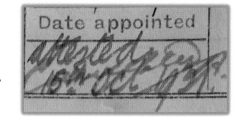

Example from married officer Lucy Charlton's file of the record of her being attested on the 15th October 1931, which was subsequently cancelled, due to Home Office regulations

This letter is included in Mrs Pearce's file because she became a widow in 1940, at which point she asked to be re-attested and have the same conditions of service as the unmarried officers.

From 1917 up to 1931 half of the female officers who had served or were still serving with the department were married. The last married officer was recruited in 1931 and the records at the museum indicate it wasn't until the 1950s that another married woman joined.

By the end of December 1931 the Chief Constable reported following further correspondence with the Home Office with respect to this matter, and stated that the amendment of the conditions of service of police women to comply with the instructions of the Home Office was now receiving attention. It was resolved that the Chief Constable be authorised to revise the conditions and that the town clerk submit the revised scale of pay allowances and conditions of service of the women police to the Home Office for approval.[108]

The marriage ban was relaxed in several forces during the Second World War. The first few female officers recruited in the 1930s and 1940s in Wolverhampton Borough Police got married whilst serving during the war and continued to serve, with no pressure to resign.

In April 1932 the Birmingham Chief Constable was considering the question of the payment of female watchers and searchers with a view to securing uniformity in practice on the various divisions (remember only 10 years earlier the work of the female watchers had been scaled back and the decision was made to only utilise them in 'special cases', not all attempted suicides). The Judicial Sub-Committee asked him to consider the matter further. This was resolved at a subsequent meeting on 27th April 1932 with payments agreed as follows[109]:

- 1/- for first hour of watching

- 9d for each subsequent hour

- 1/- for searching

Interestingly male officers would carry out this work for males who had attempted suicide, but females were still employed solely for this purpose, rather than the women police.

By the start of 1932 the caseload decreased for the first time, going down to 3,266 in 1931. It is noted that some of the Birmingham City Police special constables were included in the many people applying for help with boots and clothing. The very admirable quality of special constables of their willingness to carry out policing duties for no payment is even nobler here, when they have insufficient means to feed and clothe their family.

The department increased by five officers however one resigned that year due to ill health, making a total of 10 officers and one sergeant.

With the increase in staff, Sergeant Miles reports being able to increase patrol hours – starting earlier and visiting more locations. One officer is provided every day as court matron and three days a week one is provided as relief matron at the lock-up.

At this time the work of the women police is described by the Chief Constable as 'chiefly amongst girls who have not been convicted, but who are getting into evil courses. They make every effort to get these young girls to give up immoral lives, and take up legitimate employment, which they assist them to obtain'.[110]

During 1932 the caseload was on the increase again – up to 3,364. Figures from this year show that 34% of the cases were dealt with using institutions such as hostels, the workhouse or hospitals. Only a third were now visitors to the police station at Newton Street asking for advice.

Unmarried pregnant women were again increasing in numbers, with 50% being under the age of 18 and many from respectable homes.

More people were now starting to apply for assistance (food and clothes) for themselves and their children, often for the first time due to changes in their employment situation.

The responsibilities of the 10 constables and one sergeant were listed as follows:

- 2 patrol the outlying districts
- 2 patrol the streets and visit public places
- 4 are employed at the lock-up, one court matron and one relief matron
- 1 attends a relief depot 5 mornings a week
- Attendance at Assizes, Sessions, Adoption Court and Children's Court

The girls at the hostel were still having their interests looked after by Miss Wilson through the Ladies Advisory Committee and the Judicial Sub-Committee: in 1932 she requested that they have a wireless set and in 1933 a 'Singer sewing machine at an estimated cost of £8.6.0'. Both were approved by the sub-committee.[111]

In January 1933 the future of the role of lock-up matron was in doubt. The Chief Constable reported to the Judicial Sub-Committee on the increasing expenditure of police women and explained that it was necessary to consider replacing the matrons with policewomen. The dock matron had recently retired and the main lock-up matron was 'getting old and may have to retire at any time'.[112] He thought it much better these positions were filled by policewomen permanently, as they already had to provide the support of one policewoman at the lock-up every night.

The report for 1933 demonstrates another small increase in cases. This year 36 cases were noted where children were found wandering the streets and brought back to the office, many under the age of four. Often it would be many hours before parents or friends came to claim them.

In February 1933 the Chief Constable made an application to the Home Office for their approval to the appointment of three further women police and stated that he desired, pending their reply, to recruit to two of the vacancies.[113] The report for 1933 shows that one additional constable was recruited this year bringing the total in the department up to 12.

In April 1933 a letter was received from the Home Office with accompanying regulations amending the Police Regulations and the Police (Women) Regulations which the Secretary of State had made under the Police Act 1919. These regulations were mainly concerned with rates of pay and deductions and introduced a new scale of pay for women constables appointed since the 30th September 1931.

The Chief Constable was asked to review and 'arrange for effect to be given thereto where necessary.'[114]

In May 1933 the matter of pay for female officers was deferred to a special sub-committee and Miss Wilson was co-opted onto this committee for consideration of the matter.[115]

14th June 1933 proposals received from the special sub-committee in relation to the amended regulations were forwarded to the Home Secretary, with a view to gaining his support in the application of a new scale of pay for female officers under the regulations received back in April.'[116]

Watch Committee minutes in July 1933[117] list the items of uniform worn by the Women Police along with the prices. This includes:

- Blouses at 9/3d
- Collars at 7/6d
- Ties at 16/6d
- 20 pairs of white gloves at 20/-
- 10 pairs of black gloves at 1/9d

Total cost of these items for the whole unit was £20.7.1.

The role of women police and how their work was carried out was still expanding. In September 1933 Sergeant Miss Bushnell (lady enquiry officer from CID) made an application to the Watch Committee for 5/- per week motorcar allowance. It was resolved that the Chief Constable arrange payment.[118]

Significant legislation that affected the role of female police officers was passed in 1933. The Children and Young Persons Act (1933) gave police the power to remove young people and take them to a place of safety for protection from moral danger (amongst other things). Previously the police (more specifically the women police) had to wait for behaviour to become criminal if a young person did not wish to take them up on their advice, before they had any power to intervene. The National Council of Women petitioned for a female officer to be present in court in all cases where children were required to attend but this was turned down. Instead a requirement was passed that all children in court must be under the care of a woman, as reported in Police Orders 5th October 1933[119]:

'Also a female prisoner, under 17, while so

detained, conveyed or waiting shall be under the care of a women. Arrangements to ensure above should be made in every case.'

Another development in 1933 was a review of the provisions of section 4 of the Vagrancy Act 1824, particularly in its application in ensuring young adults could be assisted. This filled another gap in the role of the women police and their ability to address the problems presented to them, as the Children and Young Persons Act only catered for children under the age of 17.

After a number of years developing the site, Steelhouse Lane Police Station finally opened its doors at the end of November 1933[120]. It is recorded in 1930 that the Watch Committee approved the sum of £73,000 to be spent on the erection of the new central police station and offices[121] – that is the equivalent of around £4 million in today's sterling. One of the reasons for the new station was the issue of having to take prisoners to the Newton Street basement office where the A division were based, then walk them through the streets to the lock-up on Steelhouse Lane (which originally opened in the 1890s). The Women Police had their own, self-contained offices in the basement area of the new station, believed to have been entered through the central door on this picture, which shows how the building looked in 2017:

Police Orders for 23rd November 1933 state:

New Police Station, Steelhouse Lane.

The offices of the Police Women, the public carriage department, and the Lost Property Office have now been transferred from their old premises to the new Police Station in Steelhouse Lane, where all communications should be addressed in future for these departments.

These offices are connected up with the Central Police Exchange, and with the Dictograph system; and the new Telephone extension numbers will be issued in Police order in due course.

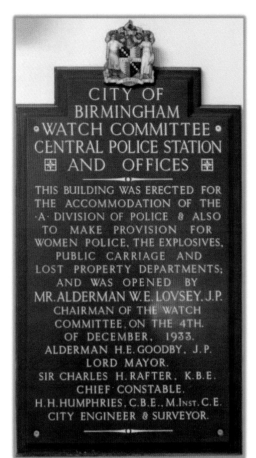

CITY OF BIRMINGHAM
• WATCH COMMITTEE •
CENTRAL POLICE STATION
⊞ AND OFFICES ⊞

THIS BUILDING WAS ERECTED FOR
THE ACCOMMODATION OF THE
·A· DIVISION OF POLICE & ALSO
TO MAKE PROVISION FOR
WOMEN POLICE, THE EXPLOSIVES,
PUBLIC CARRIAGE AND
LOST PROPERTY DEPARTMENTS;
AND WAS OPENED BY
MR. ALDERMAN W.E. LOVSEY. J.P.
CHAIRMAN OF THE WATCH
COMMITTEE. ON THE 4TH.
OF DECEMBER, 1933.
ALDERMAN H.E. GOODBY, J.P.
LORD MAYOR.
SIR CHARLES H. RAFTER, K.B.E.
CHIEF CONSTABLE.
H. H. HUMPHRIES, C.B.E., M.INST. C.E.
CITY ENGINEER & SURVEYOR.

Plaque commemorating the opening of Steelhouse Lane police station, note the women police being mentioned as some of the first occupants

The next mention of Steelhouse Lane in Police Orders, whilst being rather amusing, is also open to debate as to exactly what the problem was that was being addressed, was it the male use of the 'special occasion' female toilets, or the state they left them in?

NEW POLICE STATION, STEELHOUSE LANE.

LADIES LAVATORY.

The Ladies lavatory adjoining the Club Room must be kept locked and the key will be kept by the Sergeant in the office. Men parading must use the lavatory in the passage of the basement. The ladies' lavatory is for special occasions.[122]

1934 saw another rise in cases with a total of 3,943 being recorded.

One clear increase was in the number of visits the officers were making at the request of concerned parents or friends – up from 590 to 648. A large number of these were girls between 12 and 14 who were completely 'out of parental control'. Many of them went on to appear before a juvenile court and were sent to approved schools.

Women involved in prostitution or simply found regularly associating with different men are still referred to as 'leading immoral lives' and there is clearly a concern for the welfare of their children. Many of these are taken to training schools, orphanages or the workhouse.

During the previous year assistance was given in 521 cases whereby food, clothing and/or boots were handed out to needy women and families. This year the number dropped to 456, perhaps showing an improvement in employment circumstances for many families.

Interestingly 11 cases are reported of child neglect that were referred to the National Society for the Prevention of Cruelty to Children (NSPCC). Nowadays the NSPCC is one of many agencies referring cases to the police, rather than the other way around.

It is reported that the Women Police were instrumental in tracing many missing girls from other towns and from Birmingham itself – demonstrating an increase in more traditional police and detective work.

A great many girls aged 17 and under were still finding themselves pregnant after apparently travelling outside the city with motorists who provided false details. Sergeant Miles still highlights that the girls are often respectable and from good homes.

An insight is given into the cause of marital problems at the time whereby it is highlighted that many of the couples the female officers visit following allegations from either husband or wife stem from a lack of employment and insufficient funds coming into the home.

In April 1934 alterations were being made to the basement office at Steelhouse Lane Police Station which was occupied by the Women Police. There is talk of a sink being installed and the city surveyor being asked to send a representative to meet with the Chief Constable to determine the best arrangement.[123]

The department increased to a total of 14 (including the sergeant) and duties included providing matron cover for the lock-up and also escorting any female prisoners arrested on warrant from another town or city, as well as those held in other Birmingham stations, in to the central lock-up.

They continued to try and keep a record of all the individuals they dealt with and follow up wherever possible. It is recorded that many letters of thanks were received.

This year, as in every previous year's report, Sergeant Miles goes on to say she would like it recorded that her officers have worked incredibly hard and carried out their duties in a most effective and satisfactory matter.

In October 1934 it is reported at the Watch Committee meeting that a Mrs Mitchell had died. She is reported to have been the first female member of the Watch Committee and she also sat on the Ladies Advisory Committee for the girls' hostel. The Cecilia Martin Mitchell Memorial Fund was set up in her name and in December the Watch Committee pledged £5.[124]

A pay rise was on the cards for the Women Police from October 1934 – at the Watch Committee it was approved that the Chief Constable would ask the Home Office if he could increase the pay of women constables in Birmingham as follows:

(a) Five constables to get a pay rise from 70/- to 80/- per week subject to five per cent deduction, making the amount receivable 76/- per week

(b) Two constables to get a pay rise from 56/- per week to 62/- per week, 58/11d per week once 5 per cent deduction made[125]

In December 1934 rent allowance for policewomen was agreed at 4/- per week (single sergeants and constables) and 7/- for inspectors.[126]

By the end of 1935 the caseload has again increased up to 4,273 - the highest number recorded so far.

Cases are broken down as follows:

256	Girls and women taken to the police hostel (including 8 young children and 4 babies)
108	Girls and women taken to other hostels and shelters
80	Girls and women were found employment
582	Visits made to homes of girls interviewed at the police station following complaints by parents or friends
57	Girls reported missing were found
167	Girls and women taken to hospital (including 25 who were mentally defective and 63 suffering from venereal disease)
98	Pregnant cases taken to various institutions
36	Children sent to various homes (e.g. Barnardos, Public Assistance Home and religious institutions) and 10 cases of neglect reported to the NSPCC
60	Lost children found on the streets and children whose mothers had been arrested for shoplifting
465	Cases of assistance with food, clothing and/or boots
1,106	Homes visited or husband and wife interviewed at the office regarding marital disputes or complaints made
1,258	Persons called at the station for advice on all subjects

The complaints from husbands and wives were again on the increase, although Sergeant Miles still felt the female officers were able to play a significant part in achieving the reconciliation of many couples.

A lot of support continued to be given in the form of providing matrons for the lock-up and the support was still given to the Police Aided Association in distributing food and clothing.

On the 25th August 1935 the man who introduced policewomen to the Birmingham Police force died. Sir Charles Haughton Rafter passed away whilst on holiday in Ireland. By then he was 75 years old and had completed an astounding 52 years' police service.

On the 1st September 1935 Mr Cecil Moriarty was appointed Chief Constable. He was to head Birmingham City Police into yet another World War.

20 women are showing in the museum's records as having joined in the 1930s. Several were from Scotland and many were from far away cities and counties including Manchester, Wrexham, Blackburn and Yorkshire. Only five of them were local. In 1930, at age 24, Joan Alexander became the first woman to be recruited under the age of 30. By 1934, two 22-year-olds had been recruited and it turns out that the majority of the women (14 of the 20) recruited in this decade were in their 20s, bringing the average age of a Birmingham City policewoman down considerably. This demonstrates the effect of the 1931 regulations.

One transferee is recorded for the 1930s – Norah Gray joined from Sheffield City Police. Five of the women were previously nurses/matrons, several worked in administrative roles and three recorded their occupation as student or scholar.

In 1935 Sergeant Miles received the King George V Jubilee Medal and she held a party with the Women Police and her daughter to celebrate:

Women Police Department in 1935, published in West Midlands Police's 'Beacon' Magazine c1980. From left to right: Sergeant Tantrum, PW Ross, PW Pearce, PW Downey, PW Vernon, PW Hancox, PW Charlton, Sgt Miles, PW Porter, PW Dugard, PW Slater, PW Hale, PW Schipper, Miss Miles (Sergeant Miles' daughter), believed to be Gladys Taylor.

By 1938 signs were showing of a declining economy – now 620 cases were reported where assistance was given. Many of the other figures remained stable.

It is noted that several of the women taken to hospital the previous year were suffering from scabies or other infectious diseases.

A further problem was that many parents were in arrears and could not afford to pay their rent, which subsequently led to them being evicted and the children being sent to children's homes or similar institutions.

In a report to the 'Chairman and members of the Watch Committee'[127] dated February 21st 1938, Chief Constable Moriarty makes reference to the authorised strength of the Women Police being two inspectors, two sergeants and 13 constables (although only one inspector was in post at this time). He stated that the pay of male inspectors starts at £325 up to a maximum of £375 after five years' service, whereas the pay for women inspectors is £260 up to a maximum of £300 after four years' service.

By January 1939 the total cases recorded were 4,352 – another record breaking year - and the number of women employed by the department is 13 including the sergeant.

13 women left during the 1930s – some of these were the first officers of the department such as Evelyn Miles in 1939 who had done so much for the advancement of women in the police service. Five of those that

left during this decade did so with an ill-health pension. This demonstrates the aging workforce of women in their 50s, 60s and 70s that was starting to be rejuvenated with women in their 20s during this decade. Excluding the lady enquiry officers, no new female officers were recruited during the 1920s, hence the workforce from 1917-1919 (which was already largely in their 40s and 50s) was approaching their 60s and 70s by the end of the 1930s. Of the others - three officers left to get married, one for family reasons, one was dismissed following a disciplinary and one wanted a change of career.

Only two of these 20 women were married upon joining, in contrast to half of the women police from the 1920s. In all of the records that are held by the museum only four married women achieved the rank of sergeant (all four married to police officers) and none of the higher ranking officers ever got married. Of all of the officers who attained the rank of sergeant or above, only one was married when they joined and one was widowed, all the rest were single. In those days for women who wanted to climb the ranks, the police service was not just a job or a career but a life choice.

The average length of police career for women who joined in the 1930s was nine years and 11 months. This does not do justice to some of the longest serving women from this era – including Norah Gray who retired as a superintendent after 34 years' service, Agnes Tantrum who retired after 26 as a temporary chief inspector or Florence Schipper who retired after 30 years as a sergeant. The shortest length of service at this time was six months.

By 1939 only 45 of the 183 police forces across the country employed women police officers.[128]

Birmingham Women Police Department and Lady Enquiry Officers 1936

Standing L to R Agnes Ross, Ivy Dugard, Alice Turner, Insp Florence Mildred White (CID), Florence Schipper, Insp Susan Palmer, Bessie Hale, Sgt Doris Bushnell (CID), Janet Pollock Porter, Gladys Taylor

Seated L to R Sarah Hancox, Catherine Downey, Ellen Vernon, Sgt Evelyn Miles, Lucy Charlton, Adelaide Pearce, Agnes Tantrum

Wolverhampton Borough Police's female officers

Wolverhampton Borough Police recruited its first female officer in 1937 – some 20 years after the success in Birmingham.

Hannah Esther Bronwen Evans joined as a lady enquiry officer in the Wolverhampton CID on the 5th April 1937. She was 24 years old, came from Carmarthenshire and was paid 56/- a week. She received two commendations for work leading to arrests of abortionists & one for detection of larceny. She also completed three months detective training with the Birmingham Police Training School in Digbeth upon joining.

Interestingly Hannah got married in 1940 but remained with the force for a further 12 months before leaving in November 1941, which would indicate that Wolverhampton Borough Police had relaxed the marriage ban during the Second World War. Only three of the Wolverhampton women police were married when they joined, but many of them got married whilst working for the force.

Hannah's husband Richard Howard Bentley Page had a glowing career in the Armed Forces – he was a member of the elite Special Operations Executive during WW2 and received the MBE for his work.

Hannah's daughter Jill states family legend has it that Hannah was actually the first female detective who was a university graduate in the country. After she left the police she joined the Women's Royal Auxiliary Air Force in the Special Investigations Branch and reached the rank of Squadron Officer. After the war Hannah's husband returned to his pre-war teaching job and the couple owned a small farm. After spending four years working on the farm, Hannah too began a teaching job, but sadly died when Jill was only 23. Jill states that Hannah and Richard were very devoted and wrote many letters to each other as Richard was travelling all over the world during the war.

Hannah was joined in January 1940 by 26 year old Edith Mary Newbrook who also started on 56/- a week. Edith also got married whilst working for the police in 1943 – she married Siwert Mulder who came from Amsterdam, and became Edith Mulder. She would appear to be the first Wolverhampton female officer to go out on patrol and remained with the force until 1947.

There are a total of 32 female officers showing in the museum records as working for Wolverhampton Borough Police (including two who went on to work for West Midlands Constabulary after the 1966 amalgamation). Whilst this seems low, it isn't altogether surprising considering the first only came in 1937 and Wolverhampton Borough Police only existed for another 29 years until the amalgamation in 1966 and it was a small force in comparison to Birmingham City Police.

Three transferred, another had their services dispensed with and the rest resigned. Only one is shown as reaching the rank of sergeant although another transferred to that rank in a different force. CID and Patrol were the most common roles, although the female officers were also posted to A, B and C divisions.

Two of the officers were commended by the Chief Constable of Birmingham City Police for arresting a man for indecent assault who violently resisted arrest. A total of ten of the women received commendations either from the Watch Committee or Chief Constable.

The vast majority of the women had previous occupations – six were cadets, most were clerical (shorthand typists, telephonists, clerks etc) and two transferred from the Women's Auxiliary Police. One of the cadets from 1961 originated from Taunton. She was so keen to become a cadet, she wrote to the Home Office to enquire as to which forces across the country employed them (12 as it turned out) and subsequently wrote to each one asking if there were vacancies. At the time, only Walsall and Wolverhampton had vacancies so she applied to both and got accepted by Wolverhampton.

The average age was 23 – there were only two officers younger than 20 (both 19 – in 1953 and 1965) and two older than 26 (one aged 32 in 1944 and one aged 45 in 1953).

During the 1950s and 60s the Chief Constable of Wolverhampton was struggling to recruit and retain female officers. He found a couple of candidates who were 19 years of age who he wanted to recruit immediately so he wrote to the Home Office to ask for permission to recruit them under Regulation 7 (Police Regulations 1965) as they were under the required age of 20. Permission was given and they started straight away.

Only one sergeant is recorded – Mavis Lavinia Vaughan, nee Williams. Born in 1934, she joined in 1957 and potentially went on to become Wolverhampton Borough's first and only female sergeant. She left in November 1963, shortly before the force was amalgamated. She was commended on one occasion where she was awarded a certificate of merit by the Watch Committee for her part in the arrest of violent hooligan.

The average length of career was four years and three months. The longest was 13 years and 10 months and the shortest just over seven months. Only two of the female officers files held at the museum for Wolverhampton Borough continued past April 1966 into West Midlands Constabulary.

Coventry City Police's female officers

The topic of women police appears in the Watch Committee minutes in Coventry in 1919. Due to the success of the Voluntary Women's Patrols in the area, the secretary of the Coventry branch of the National Council of Women asked if the appointment of women police was being considered as 'social workers in the city felt strongly that the presence of fully trained and qualified women police would be of great benefit to the wellbeing of the citizens'. The Watch Committee however, had no intention of considering any such thing.[129]

Once in 1924 and twice during 1934 the question of women police was again brought to the Watch Committee but they would not reverse their decision – despite the issuance of Home Office regulations on the conditions of employment and two Government Commissions recommending an increase in numbers of policewomen.

In 1935 the Watch Committee held a vote on a recommendation that women police would NOT be appointed with 23 to 19 voting in favour of them not being appointed. It would be another three years before Coventry would appoint its first female police officers.

Minutes from the committee in September 1937 show that they were starting to consider how women police could be usefully employed, particularly in dealing with women, girls and juvenile offenders. The success of women matrons in dealing with female prisoners is mentioned and a recommendation was passed for two women constables to be appointed in April 1938, subject to approval from the Secretary of State.[130]

This was approved and on 25th April 1938 two female officers were recruited – Ena Goodacre and Kathleen Rowe. In their report to the Watch Committee in November 1939,[131] they outline the work they have carried out so far. This starts with their training at the Birmingham Police Training School which included the standard training for male recruits, but also additional training with the Women Police and the lady enquiry officers based within the Birmingham CID. They learned how to take statements and received advice in how to interview women and girls regarding sexual offences.

After completion of their training in July 1938 they returned to Coventry and during their first year:

- Interviewed 1,048 women and girls
- Took 277 statements
- Acted as escort to 53 women and girls
- Made 32 arrests

The women highlight that much of their work related to parents asking them for advice, claiming their daughters were out of control and they didn't know what to do. A lot of referrals were also made to the policewomen in relation to girls and women in need of help, lodgings and/or employment. This is very similar to the early years of the Birmingham City Women Police where their work consisted mainly of assisting with social welfare issues.

The women state that the escort duties they carried out included taking women and girls to various hostels, remand homes and prisons.

Interestingly they include the Birmingham Police Women's Hostel (which would have been Newton Street by this time) as one of the recipients of the women they assisted.

The report goes on to say:

'The arrests have chiefly been for shop-lifting, although there have been a number of girls arrested and charged with being in need of care and protection, or in moral danger.

For the first three months of our work here, there was some reluctance on the part of the public to bring matters to our notice. This has considerably altered. Whereas in the first three months of our work we interviewed 146 women and girls, in the last three months we have interviewed 252.

In addition to our work in connection with women and girls, we have spent considerable lengthy periods in observation work on I.R.A. activities, indecency complaints, and on periodical complaints of thefts from the person.

During the first few months of our work, we spent considerable periods patrolling public parks and commons, and also visited the various Women's lavatories, with a certain amount of success, but owing to the above observations which took up some of our time, we had to somewhat curtail these, but we hope in the near future to give more attention to this.'

Ena was born in 1911 and spent her early years on her family's farm. She had an interest in rifles from an early age and used to practise target shooting with an air rifle. After joining Coventry City Police in 1938, she became the force's first female sergeant in December 1943.

After the war she joined the Probation Service and in 1957 moved to Vancouver, Canada, where she picked up another accolade – British Colombia's first female probation officer. She returned to England in 1963, continuing to work in the Probation Service until she retired in 1976. She joined a local shooting club and won many trophies. She was also part of a British shooting team sent to Canada in 1974. In 1988 she again made history by being the National Rifle Association's Captain of the British ladies team sent to compete against Australia. This was the first and only time the British NRA sent a women's fullbore rifle team to any overseas championships. Ena was very much respected for her wisdom and calming influence, as well as her non-judgmental insight into people and events. She never married and died on February 24th 2008[132].

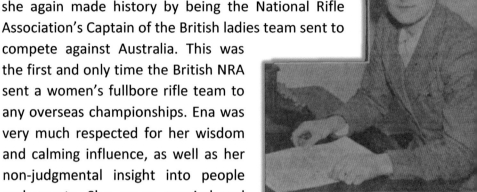

Ena Goodacre - Coventry Evening Telegraph, 16th December 1943

Kathleen Rowe was 27 when she joined Coventry Police alongside Ena – going straight into the CID. She stated in an interview in My Weekly from June 1st 1996, that her cousin's husband encouraged her to join after seeing an article in The Police Review which said that more women were being recruited. She originally applied for the Metropolitan Police but was turned down. Their loss was Coventry's gain!

She stated she never felt opposition from her male counterparts, but felt they were always very supportive. Kathleen recalls the investigation into the 1939 IRA bombing campaign and how she spoke a lot to a female prisoner, eventually being able to convince her to give the evidence needed bring the bombers to trial.

Kathleen also recalled on other occasions where male officers were protective of her and if things got a bit heated, asked her to retreat to safety and protected her from foul language. She stated that male colleagues (and criminals!) always showed her the utmost of respect. Unlike todays policewomen dealing with riots, assaults and other dangerous situations - Kathleen stated that female officers back then were often likely to be asked to deal with drunken women! She also recalled some difficult times during the Coventry Blitz having to respond to queries from relatives asking if their family members were ok after bombing raids and trying to prevent looting. Unfortunately Police Regulations at the time meant that Kathleen was forced to retire upon her marriage four years into her service. She went on to have three children and we are thankful to Wendy and Anne for sharing details of their mother's service.

They recall she was a natural detective and transitioned perfectly into a role as a store detective after she left the police. They also remember how she would 'police' a war memorial in the city, ensuring children treated it with respect and didn't play on it. Kathleen met her husband during World War 2 when he was fire watching on the roof of the Coventry Council House – presumably narrowly missing the bomb that landed on the police station!

This group pic shows Kathleen on holiday in 1939, possibly with other members of the Coventry force and their partners. Kathleen is standing on the far left of the second row. Ena Goodacre may well be in this picture as well:

By January 1957 Inspector Mrs Joanne Green is referenced as outlining the history of the women's branch to the Watch Committee and in November 1957 she was showing visitors round the new force headquarters. Inspector Green initially spent two years with Kent County Constabulary from 1944 to 1946 and the following ten years with Rochdale Borough Police before joining Coventry City Police in June 1956. She may have been their first female inspector.

Dudley Borough Police's female officers

Dudley Borough resisted female officers for as long as possible – with Chief Constable James Niven Campbell holding out until male officers started to enlist in the Armed Forces before finally accepting they could add some value to the force.

Minutes from December 1939 show that he was 'unconvinced women could do more than a regular and special constable, and would have to be accompanied by an ordinary uniform officer.'[133] It was resolved that the views of the Chief Constable be accepted and the question of the appointment of women police be 'not entertained'.

By 1940 the Home Office was asking forces who had not yet appointed any women police to seriously consider doing so. In October, in response to a letter received back in August, the Chief Constable was finally convinced to recruit some women. He started with Women's Auxiliary Police Corps but only on a part-time, unpaid basis. With regards to paid police women, this was deferred 'until such time as there may arise a greater need for their service'.[134]

By March 1941 with a male telephone operator being called up for military service and the challenge in obtaining 'suitable youths' to employ, a suggestion to employ a woman for this role was approved.

In response to a further Home Office Circular in 1941 relating to the employment of women for certain duties in the police service, the Chief Constable recommended the appointment of three female clerks to release three constables back to other duties. However this couldn't happen right away as the women would 'require considerable training'.[135]

It wasn't until 1947 that Dudley finally recruited female officers: they were PW 1 Rooss and PW 2 Carter.

Sadly Agnes Rooss's file has not survived, but we do have Doreen Carter's and can shed a little light on her career.

Doreen Carter was living in Leeds in 1947 when she saw an advert in the local paper for policewomen in Dudley. She promptly applied, stating she had served five years in the Women's Land Army and enclosed two references, one where the War Agricultural Executive Team of the Isle of Ely highly recommended her for employment, and stated they would very much regret seeing her leave.

On the 9th of August 1947 Doreen was sworn in and her first progress report from her training at Ryton-on-Dunsmore showed she had made an exemplary start.

In 1948 she attended the Detective School in the West Riding Constabulary and again received a glowing report. In 1955 she was promoted to sergeant, potentially the first female sergeant the Dudley Borough Police had ever had.

By 1964 Doreen was back at West Riding, completing an advanced course in criminal investigation and in 1967 furthered that knowledge with another criminal investigation course at the Birmingham City Police. She was recorded as being a credit to her force and a very competent officer.

Also in 1967, whilst attending a report of children being left unattended in an apartment block, Doreen fell the last few stairs in an unlit, steep stairwell, causing her to jar her back on the stairs which caused pain in her back and difficulty breathing. Showing what sturdy stuff she was made of, Doreen did not take any sick leave to recover but carried on with her duty.

At the end of 1968, Doreen was diagnosed with pneumonia, which led to her having to take 3 months off work. After returning to work she started having to regularly assist her sister back home in Yorkshire, a widow in poor health, which meant travelling across the country as often as possible.

Combined with her own health and the pressures of police work, Doreen found she could no longer juggle all these responsibilities and gave notice of her intent to retire in September 1969.

Susan Florence Palmer was born in South Africa in 1899, but had been living in the UK for 16 years when she applied for a shorthand typist position with Birmingham City Police in 1918. When asked for a reference, initially a Mr Briggs (on behalf of her employer, the Austin Motor

Company), stated she was very good at her job and he couldn't really spare her. This led to Miss Palmer writing in to the Chief Constable stating she hoped the job would not fall through because of this and

she was sure if she requested it personally then she could secure her release. Subsequently Mr Briggs wrote again to the Chief Constable to say on further consideration they had now decided they could dispense with her services and he would have much pleasure in recommending her. This could be considered early evidence of female powers of persuasion!

So in June 1918 Miss Palmer became a lady typist and was later promoted to being the Chief Constable's private secretary, supervising all of the female staff in the force. By 1930 she became very interested in the work of the Women Police Department and successfully applied for a new role as inspector of the Women Police. On 1st April 1930 she took up the position and became the joint first female inspector in Birmingham City Police as it was also the same day Miss Florence White gained the rank of inspector as the lady enquiry officer.

In 1937 she petitioned to have her former service from 1919 (when she attained the age of 20) up to her official appointment as a member of the Women Police in 1930 included as pensionable service. This was approved by the Watch Committee on recommendation from the Chief Constable.

In 1941 Chief Constable Moriarty wrote a testimony to be placed on Inspector Palmer's file. He wrote that her services were invaluable to the previous Chief Constable Charles Haughton Rafter and were invaluable to him too. He records that as the Chief Constable's confidential secretary she was in charge of all of the female administrative staff across the force and was responsible for testing all applicants. When she joined the Women Police Department she 'greatly contributed to their successful organisation' and in addition to that she deals with the girls' hostel. In 1930 she was granted a special honorarium to recognise her hard work and efforts whilst a chief superintendent and a chief inspector were absent from the force. The Chief Constable personally applied to the Watch Committee for the recognition as he stated he could not have managed without her services.

In 1943 Inspector Palmer received the British Empire Medal and in 1946 the Defence Medal. She eventually retired in 1948, aged 48, and returned to her native South Africa. She had some difficulties sorting out the last of her tax returns and pension and the Chief Constable intervened on her behalf and personally wrote to the Home Office to address the matter.

In 1960 she was living back in the UK in Devonshire and she died in 1986.

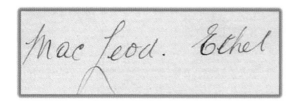

Ethel MacLeod originated from Liverpool. Born in 1897, she applied to Join Birmingham City Police in 1930 when she was 32. Checks by local police established that she was from a most respectable family and was held in the highest esteem in the locality that she resided. She revealed she was separated from her husband, a sergeant in the Royal

Air Force, due to his drinking and bad treatment of her. She had been living in India with him where he was serving but left with her two children (aged eight and four) to return to her mother's address in Liverpool.

She was accepted into the force and was a probationary constable alongside Agnes Tantrum.

In May 1933 she reported to Chief Superintendent James Burnett that her husband had been hanging around her house whilst she was on duty. Having left the RAF, he was now out of employment and staying at the Salvation Army hostel. She was scared he might cause her an injury because of his drunken habits. The chief superintendent saw her husband and told him to leave his wife alone as she was 'in a job that did not permit of scandals'. In July she informed Chief Superintendent Burnett that a friend of theirs had arrived from India and she invited him to stay with her and the children. He stayed for two weeks, leading up to a night where she arrived home from a party she had attended with the friend and another couple when her husband arrived and caused a disturbance.

Mrs McLeod was suspended from duty pending an investigation into her conduct. Her husband was seen by Inspector Palmer and he gave quite a different story. He said that her conduct with other men was the reason he turned to drink in India and that his wife was plausible and cunning. He advised he would be instituting proceedings for divorce and that he wished his wife to resign rather than be dismissed as she could then get her superannuation reductions returned and this would be better for the children.

On the 27th July 1933[136] the case was heard against police woman MacLeod in a meeting of the Watch Committee's Judicial Sub-Committee. They found her guilty of discreditable conduct in that she 'acted in a manner prejudicial to discipline and likely to bring discredit on the reputation of the Police Force by having a male person resident in her house, she being at the same time separated from her husband.'

Her suspension was lifted and she was called upon to resign. Her pension deductions of £15. 3. 2. were authorised to be returned to her. She subsequently became the first policewoman in Birmingham to be asked to resign.

 Bessie Wooden Hale was born on the 29th September 1908 in Gloucester. In February 1931 she applied to join Birmingham City Police, stating her present occupation was a ladies maid at a school. The Chief Constable replied to her and stated he was hoping to recruit shortly but that he was concerned about her age (she was 22) and enquired about what experience she might have which might help her to carry out the role of policewoman.

This highlights the significant change imposed upon the force with the 1931 regulations – prior to 1931 most of the police women recruited were married and older than 35, demonstrating the attitude of the Chief Constable at the time and the age and personal circumstances which he felt made the best police women. The regulations however meant they had to recruit unmarried women between the ages of 22 and 35, leading to a significant step change in the profile and experience of future recruits.

Bessie originally applied to join the Metropolitan Police but again they were concerned with her age and they were also apparently concerned by her height – she stated in her letter of interest she was 5'9".

The Chief Constable then wrote to Bessie to say it was usual practice to ask local police to carry out enquiries into potential new recruits and in a very considerate manner, asked if this would cause her any problems, e.g. were her employers aware she was enquiring about a new position?

Bessie was one of the first female officers to be posted out to division – she was posted to D Division in February 1940 where she remained until the end of 1942 when she applied to resign due to her planned marriage in early December. She left Birmingham City Police on the 29th November 1942.

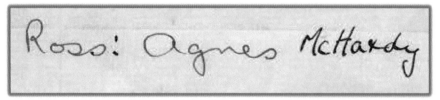

Agnes Ross was born in Edinburgh in 1896. She applied to join the Birmingham City Police whilst working as a typist in 1931. Her employer gave a glowing reference, stating she was very alert and keen and showed a strong personality which would suit a role allowing her to use her initiative and make decisions.

In a letter from the Chief Constable to Miss Ross in March 1931, he stated he could see her any day the following week for an interview. Miss Palmer from the Women Police would collect her from the train station and book her a room for the night if she so wished. Interestingly he says 'I would suggest you bring your luggage with you, so that you would not have to travel back for it, if you were appointed, after having passed the Police Surgeon'. How different from the various stages of recruitment today which can take months after showing an expression of interest to finally being selected!

She became a sergeant on the 1st January 1940 and after previously assisting Sergeant Miles for several years, took over following her retirement.

In 1951 she wrote to her chief inspector to ask that the Police Pension Regulations be waived and she be allowed to continue working past the recommended retirement age for women of 55. This was approved and she remained in force until 1956 when she completed 25 years' service.

She left the force on the 18th March 1956 and died in March 1986 aged 89.

Munton : Evelyn . Crawford

Mrs Evelyn Crawford Munton was born on 3rd March 1900. She was originally from Manchester and applied to join Birmingham City Police in May 1930. She stated she took a course of motoring after leaving school at age 16 and then joined the Women's Legion – being demobilised in 1919. For the eight years prior to her application to join the police she had been working as a chauffeuse to a private gentleman.

Through local police enquiries into her character it was established that she was a married woman, living apart from her husband. She was recruited on the 17th April 1931.

Between April and October 1931 she was admitted to hospital twice and had 11 weeks of sick leave recorded. She underwent an operation in August 1931. She was suffering from cystitis and an inflamed bladder. Two things that would potentially have been challenging for most women to discuss with male doctors at that time.

In October 1931 Mrs Munton resigned – stating her reasons as 'my prolonged illness and uncertainty of recovery'.

In December 1931 she wrote to the Chief Constable to ask for return of her superannuation contributions – thanking him for the skilled medical care she received whilst in the force and stating that her medical care was ongoing, at tremendous expense to herself.

In January 1933 the daughter of the gentleman Mrs Munton previously worked for as a chauffeuse wrote to Councillor Miss Wilson to ask if she could help to obtain a position back within the Women Police for Mrs Munton as she had now recovered. She stated Mrs Munton was of great service to her family and they were very fond of her, she had only left their service as her father unfortunately had to give up his car.

Miss Wilson duly wrote to the Chief Constable asking for him to consider the case of 'Miss' Munton. Chief Constable Rafter subsequently responded – stating he had already looked into her case but due to the introduction of the Police (Women) Regulations 1931, he could no longer employ Mrs Munton as she was a married woman.

And thus Evelyn Munton became one of the first casualties of the marriage ban imposed on female officers.

Dear Councillor Miss Wilson,

I have just received your letter of the 26th instant, about Mrs. Munton, enclosing one from Mrs. Southall.

I had already looked into her case, as promised you at the Judicial Sub-Committee. She joined here in April 1931, and resigned in October 1931, having been on the sick list for 81 days. Had she remained in the Police Force it would have been all right, but under the Police (Women) Regulations of 1931 by which we are now bound, it is impossible to engage a married woman, so that there would be no possibility for her now to get into the Women Police Force, at least until her husband dies.

You refer to her as Miss Munton, but she really is a married woman.

Yours faithfully,

Chief Constable.

Letter from Chief Constable discussing the case of Mrs Munton, who could not be re-employed following the 1931 Police (Women) Regulations as she was a married woman

Doris Gertrude Bushnell was born in Calcutta, India on the 18th April 1908. She was privately schooled in Bournemouth and later attended London's University College before studying Law at Oxford, where she applied to join Birmingham City Police in 1933.

She joined in August 1933 as a lady enquiry officer in the CID in the rank of sergeant and continued with her law studies – being called to the Bar in 1934.

By 1935 she was becoming more ambitious and applied for an external post of factory inspector but was unsuccessful. She was clearly appreciated by the force, who recognised her high levels of education and capacity, as in July 1935 the Chief Constable wrote to the Home Office asking for an additional inspector post to be added to the policewomen establishment in Birmingham so that Miss Bushnell could be promoted, but he was not successful, on the basis that it was for personal reasons – not down to the actual resource requirements.

She applied for an additional three jobs outside of the police force by 1938 but was seemingly unsuccessful in all of them. In May 1937 she requested permission to resign to take up 'other work'. Within two days and after being spoken to by a senior officer she withdrew her application.

Following the retirement of Miss White, Miss Bushnell was promoted to the rank of inspector, remaining as a lady enquiry officer in the CID.

In October 1938 she was interviewed by the Birmingham Gazette following her recent holiday to America, where she visited the famous New York Women's Prison and also met with Margaret Sullivan, head of New York's 150 strong women police.

In 1940 she took over as the inspector in charge of the Women Police following Miss Palmer's retirement.

In 1943 she applied for permission to use her personal motor car (a Morris 8) to visit women stationed out on divisions and to carry out her own enquiries. She also stated that if her request was approved, could she please be provided with coupons for the five and a half gallons of petrol needed to retrieve the car from Bournemouth!

She applied for several more jobs over the years – indeed her ambition and desire for new challenges never seemed to fade.

Records show that in March 1944 her father died and she was given three weeks compassionate leave (without pay) and a week's annual leave to attend to matters in her home town of Bournemouth. Circumstances are very different today with a variety of paid (and in certain circumstances unpaid) compassionate and special leave available.

By April 1944 she requested permission to resign as her mother was living alone in Bournemouth and she was an only child. There were no relatives or friends available to care for her and Miss Bushnell stated her mother was very attached to her home so she felt it her duty to go and live with her there. She had also managed to secure a job in Bournemouth working as a social welfare officer.

In March 1964, after having undergone a serious operation before the previous Christmas, Miss Bushnell passed away. She had previously taken up a job as a solicitor and become a justice of the peace in Bournemouth.

In May 1937 Norah Gray applied to join the Birmingham City Police. She was born in November 1906 and had served five and a half years with the Sheffield City Police. She initially applied for the position of woman enquiry officer as a vacancy had opened up with the retirement of Miss White.

By October 1941 she attained the rank of inspector and the Chief Constable decided that as well as managing her duties in the Criminal Investigation Department, she should also be the organiser of the Women's Auxiliary Police Corps – set up in 1941 and referred to in more detail later.

In 1948 she applied for a position of woman staff officer to Her Majesty's Inspectors of Constabulary. This position was advertised following Miss Barbara Mary Denis de Vitré (the previous staff officer) being appointed as the first female Assistant Inspector of Constabulary. This highlights the expansion of women into different policing roles and is another key development in the history of women in the police service. Inspector Gray did not get the position – it went to a female officer from the Metropolitan Police Service.

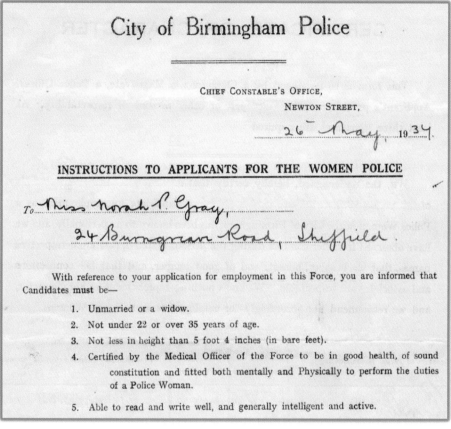

Excerpt from Norah's application form showing the recruitment criteria for Women Police

Norah Gray became the first female chief inspector in the Birmingham City Police on 1st January 1950.

In 1953 Chief Inspector Gray received the British Empire Medal for services to women police. By this time the authorised establishment of her department was 51 strong. She had received nine commendations from the Watch Committee for excellence in her work. The outstanding work and efficiency of the Women Police Department was attributed largely to her influence. In addition to her police work, she addressed many women's societies and organisations on the work of her department which no doubt helped to further their work.

She was promoted to the rank of superintendent on 1st July 1954 – becoming the first female to hold the rank in Birmingham City Police and the first outside of London. The department again increased in size – an indication that the role of female police officers was becoming more and more important in Birmingham.

In March 1960 whilst on holiday Superintendent Gray was caught up in the earthquake disaster in Agadir, Morrocco. She sustained facial injuries and a broken hip but thankfully escaped more serious injuries. Chief Constable Edward Dodd sent her the following telegram:

'DEEPLY REGRET YOUR MISFORTUNE BUT DELIGHTED TO KNOW THAT YOU ARE SAFE STOP WISH YOU SPEEDY RECOVERY STOP LET ME KNOW WHAT HELP WE CAN GIVE STOP BEST WISHES FROM ALL RANKS BIRMINGHAM CITY POLICE STOP DODD'

She eventually got to carry out the role as staff officer to HM Inspectors of Constabulary in 1960 when she was successful in applying for a one-month secondment to assist Miss Barbara de Vitre, who had by that point accomplished 14 years in post as the first female Assistant Inspector of Constabulary. Miss Gray actually stayed with the Home Office for 18 months before returning to Birmingham!

She retired from the force on the 30th June 1966 and died on the 31st August 1991 aged 84.

Margaret MacKinnon MacRae was born in Eccles, a small village in the Scottish Borders on 21st March 1907. She first applied to join the Birmingham City Police in May 1937. Her application was swiftly followed up by a letter from Sir Hugh Turnbull (Chief Constable of the City of London Police), stating a friend of his Sir Colin MacRae was interested in Margaret's application and would like to know how she is getting on. He stated 'I need hardly say I should be very happy if I learn that she has been successful in getting the post she seeks'!

Miss MacRae's application was progressing smoothly when Sir Colin MacRae wrote to enquire about the progress of his 'clanswoman'. This was followed by another letter from Sir Hugh Turnbull enquiring the same – there was certainly a lot of high profile interest in her application.

From July 1937 it would seem Miss MacRae did not pursue the application but she then writes to the Chief Constable in February 1939 stating she wishes to have an interview as she is still interested in the position of policewoman.

She subsequently started with the force in October 1939 and was complimented within the year for the arrest of a person found stealing. She was complimented on a further two occasions and highly commended on one occasion for the arrest of a person trying to steal a suitcase and its contents from New Street railway station.

In November 1944 she asked for permission to resign as she was interested in doing relief work overseas under the Council of British Societies for Relief Abroad. Her application was refused by the Chief Constable with the statement 'I cannot agree to the PW leaving the police service at the present time'. At this point the strength of the force was severely depleted due to the Second World War and the Women Police Department were carrying out a lot of war work on behalf of the Government.

By April 1945 she applied again – this time stating 'I am anxious to join the staff of Welfare Officers in the West Indies appointed by the English Colonial Office… Owing to my age, I understand I cannot apply for this position later on, as I shall then be too old.'

It would appear that she wasn't successful as in 1946, still with the force, she applied for a role as a probation officer. She subsequently resigned from the force before being appointed elsewhere – stating she had no more interest in police work.

In October 1946 the Chief Constable received a letter from the Colonial Office in London stating that Miss MacRae's sister was travelling to Trinidad to undertake hospital work and she wished to take Miss MacRae with her, so enquiries were being made about her employment prospects. The letter stated that the proposal for women police in Trinidad was again under active discussion and they wanted to know if Miss MacRae would be able to help, not just as a policewoman, but to actually help set up the service. The Chief Constable replied that she did not undertake any promotion exams whilst in Birmingham but that he thought she would be suitably qualified for the role and her experience in Birmingham was wide ranging and would stand her in good stead. The reply from the Colonial Office thanked the Chief Constable for replying so fully and helpfully, and stated that 'it is characteristic of the Birmingham Police Force'!

Elizabeth Sophia Ashcroft was born in October 1879 in Thornbury, Gloucestershire. She married Thomas James Raymont on July 26th 1904, in Warwickshire.

In December 1923 Mrs Raymont wrote to the Chief Constable asking if she could gain a position at the lock-up on Newton Street as she had heard there was a vacancy. She stated she was the widow of the late PC A49 Raymont and she had three children to support – aged eight, 16 and 18. She went on to say she was quite without resource with the exception of the gratuity given by the Watch Committee.

Her late husband Thomas joined Birmingham City Police on 20th December 1902 at 21 and a half years old.

He was complimented on four occasions and awarded a guinea each time for good police work in catching warehouse breakers, a thief trying doors at night and the arrest of burglars.

He died on 3rd September 1919 aged 38.

In her file is a report of duties of the existing matrons Lipscombe and Childs which was shared with her to inform her what the role would entail:

'The matrons' hours of duty are 8-4, 4-10 and 10-8. They take their turn in weekly order and get one day off per week. Their role is to look after female prisoners, escort them in the van from police station to lock-up when required, take their fingerprints if necessary and assist kitchen staff to prepare meals for prisoners.

Miss Chapman is classed as a policewoman and is returned by Mrs Miles on her morning state. She works 9-5, always has Sundays off and is always accompanied by one of the matrons.
Her main duty is to be with female prisoners in court and she also looks after female prisoners, helps with fingerprints and meals.

The pay of the matrons is:
- Lipscombe 27/- and 7/- war bonus per week
- Childs 25/- and 7/- war bonus per week
- Chapman 25/- and 7/- war bonus per week

Policewomen starting pay is 50/- per week, rising to 65/- in 9 years.'

Over the next 20 years she reported sick a total of 10 times, often for a month or two at a time, suffering from flu, ear trouble, tonsillitis, and a sprained knee when trying to catch a prisoner who had fallen.

There is much documentation in her file from the Second World War regarding her missing lectures where participants undertook gas mask training - testing their respirators and smelling different gas samples. At this point she had a goitre on her neck which she claimed made her unable to wear a respirator. It is referred to as a disability by one senior officer reporting on the matter. She later saw the police surgeon who reported he could not advise her to wear a gas mask under the circumstances. This could be considered as one of the very first examples of the police force making a reasonable adjustment.

She was eventually medically retired on the 26th February 1942 following a visit to the police surgeon. He stated she was incapacitated and unable to carry out her role and this was likely to be permanent.

There is also interesting documentation at the end of her file relating to sickness benefit before she retired. As was the practice at the time, Mrs Raymont received sickness benefit from her insurance company and the force deducted the same from her wages. There is a letter from the force accountant asking why Prudential had only been paying her recent sickness benefit at 10/- per week when the rate for widows was 15/-, which is what the force had deducted from her wages. They wrote back to say it was because she had reached 60 years of age and was 'therefore only entitled to 10/- per week.' Clearly reaching that milestone meant she did not need those extra five shillings!

She died in June 1955 in Birmingham, at the age of 75.

There is very little mention of other matrons after Mrs Raymont left other than the Chief Constable writing to former policewoman Lucy

Charlton in 1944 to ask if she wanted to fill a vacancy in the lock-up and much later, a report to the Watch Committee in November 1965 stating that the seven matrons currently employed in the central lock-up provide insufficient cover and an eighth was requested to be recruited[137]. The file for Elizabeth Raymont is the only personal file of a lock-up matron that has survived.

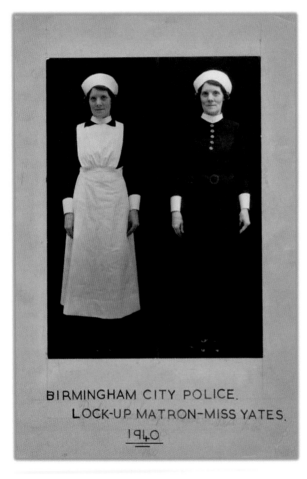

BIRMINGHAM CITY POLICE.
LOCK-UP MATRON–MISS YATES.
1940

A rare picture of a lock-up matron, and one who probably worked alongside Mrs Raymont – Miss Yates

The Second World War and the Women Police

On the 3rd of September 1939 Britain was again at war. The First World War had only ended 20 years earlier and was therefore still a recent memory. Terror gripped the nation as a German onslaught was predicted with high explosive and gas attacks being feared. Residents of Birmingham settled into the routine of constant air raid drills and carrying gas masks everywhere with them.

It has often been said that the working people of Birmingham were the first to know when war with Germany was inevitable. The First World War had been fought as Birmingham v. Krupp as Birmingham produced vast quantities of munitions for our forces just as the Krupp Company produced munitions for Germany. This was repeated leading up to the Second World War. By 1937 in Birmingham the work force would have noticed a change from commodity production to the production of war materials[138].

Birmingham City Police celebrated its centenary in 1939. It would seem that this passed without incident - perhaps the thought of another war devastating another generation distracted the authorities from the opportunity to celebrate with the pomp and ceremony one would have expected.

Remembering the sudden rush of men to the colours in the first war, the Secretary of State wrote to the Birmingham Watch Committee and told them that police officers should be discouraged from enlisting because experienced men would serve the state more usefully by continuing with police duty. Recruitment was suspended for the duration of the war and the police officers were given 'reserved occupation status.' Of course men would still enlist as we will cover later and additional war duties would be undertaken by the Special Constabulary, Police Auxiliary Messengers, the Women's Auxiliary Police Corps (WAPC), the First Police Reserve and Police War Reserve Constables.

Birmingham City Police were, as you would expect, to play a key role in the protection of Birmingham.

Birmingham City Police Headquarters at this time was situated on the end of Newton Street (number 55) on the corner of Steelhouse Lane, opposite the police run women's hostel at 58 Newton Street. The former headquarters is now used by the courts. In preparation for the air raids the cellar in the police building was surrounded by sand bags at ground level and the cellar was fortified to be used as a war room.

From February 1940 one policewoman had been attached to each of the B, C, D and E divisions due to the expansion in the use of policewomen in general police duties. The role policewomen were to play in the air raids was significant and they played a vital role in the co-ordination of the wardens, rescue parties and co-ordination of bomb damage. It was important to have policewomen available and close enough that in the event of an air raid they could be on duty very quickly. The answer was to empty the hostel and use it for the accommodation of 12 police women and later, two of the women's auxiliary officers.

By April 1941 heavy bombing was being experienced right across the Midlands, but particularly in Birmingham and Coventry. During the war there were to be 16 police officers killed in the Coventry force and 17 war related deaths within the Birmingham City Police. On the night of the 8th April into the morning of the 9th April, the police station on St. Mary's Street in Coventry City Centre took a direct hit and four officers lost their lives – Special Constable Frank Henry Kimberley, Specials Commander Arthur Frederick Matts MBE, Special Constable Thomas Arthur Harroway and Special Constable Harold Leslie Lowe who was found the following day in the wreckage.

Rescue workers searching through the wreckage of Coventry's Central Police Station in St Mary Street, Coventry.

Former Coventry Police Station in 2017

This brings us to evening and early hours of the 9th/10th April 1941. When the sirens sounded it is safe to assume that the policewomen occupied the `war room'. The raid intensified and it was clear that the central area of Birmingham was the target. As the drone of enemy aircraft neared and the sound of exploding bombs grew louder one wonders what went through the minds of those police women on duty. With little more than a few sand bags and a tin helmet separating them from oblivion they remained at their post.

Tin police helmet used during Second World War

During this air raid central Birmingham suffered severe damage in and around the Bull Ring and markets area. PC Gready was on duty at Digbeth Police Station and was killed when a bomb dropped at that location. Newton Street was also in the firing line. At 1.05am at least two bombs fell. The mortuary was completely destroyed. Severe damage was caused to the Chief Constable's office situated on the 2nd floor of the police headquarters and the building had to be made safe.

Bomb damage to Newton Street

Several other buildings suffered blast damage with smashed windows and roof tiles being blown clean off, including the Victoria Law Courts, the superintendents' flats, the Coroner's Court, Forensic Science Laboratory, Juvenile Court and the girls' hostel. The raid caused minimal disruption to the policing of the city but unfortunately another officer was lost. Detective Inspector Mark William Sellek was on fire-watching duty on the roof of the police building in Newton Street when the air raid took place and died as a result of this enemy action. Special Constable Frank Cook (and with him his wife and their three day old baby), Special Constable Ralph Wilkinson and Special Constable Rowland Harman also lost their lives that night.

Bomb damaged police HQ then and now – the new brickwork is clearly visible on the building

Newton Street – girl's hostel on the end of the street on the left just past the man with the bicycle in the first picture, police headquarters on the right – and below in 2017

Throughout the war over 127,140 enquiries were received by the military authorities. These enquiries concerned absenteeism, welfare, family circumstances and compassionate leave and were undertaken for the most part by women police officers. During the war a supplementary allowance of 5/- per week non-pensionable was paid to constables and 4/- women police, to compensate for the rise in the cost of living and to make comparability with civilian pay. A war duty allowance was also paid of 3/- per week for constables and 4/- for sergeants, with an allowance of 3/- for both ranks of women police.

This picture showa some women entering the bomb site – complete with skirts and heels! It is likely these were members of the Women Police.

In 1945 World War Two ended and the nation started the long process of rebuilding. This had been a different kind of war on an even bigger industrial scale than the first. World War One had been largely fought in foreign fields. This war had been very different, not only had it cost the lives of thousands of young men and women overseas but the population on the Home Front had also suffered under the rain of high explosive bombs from above and rationing would go on for some years yet. At the outset of the war the authorised establishment of Birmingham City Police was 1,888. Throughout the Second World War 500 men were to join the armed forces. In the annual report by the Chief Constable in 1945 he announced 'I deeply regret to record that 44 men were killed on active service or their death presumed and five died whilst serving in the Armed Forces.[139]

The men returned from war and the ranks of the regular police started to return to some resemblance of pre-war establishment but more needed to be done to reach this figure. The force advertised for recruits and wages increased but Birmingham failed to reach anywhere near full establishment. Recruitment and retention of staff was to be a problem for many years yet. More men were leaving than were joining due to retirement, lack of wages and difficulty of adjusting back into peace time roles. The same cannot be said for police women and by the end of 1946 the establishment of women stood at 22, being made up of two inspectors, five sergeants and 15 constables.

The Women's Auxiliary Police (1941-1946)

The wartime organisation perhaps most relevant to this book was the Women's Auxiliary Police Corps (WAPC). On the 29th October 1941 the Corps were established in Birmingham. They were disbanded on the 31st March 1946 and the maximum strength achieved was 142[140].

On 1st October 1941 upon promotion to inspector, Norah Gray was appointed organiser of the Women's Auxiliary Police. She continued to manage this department upon her promotion to Head of the Women's Police Department in April 1944.

The initial recruitment was set at 50 women to be paid at £2.7s.0d per week. They were engaged in full-time roles as drivers, shorthand typists, clerks and telephonists. Duties included manning the front desk (an ironic turn of phrase!), assisting with CID administrative work, patrolling the streets of Birmingham and mobile patrol. They did not wear a police uniform as such but dressed in a dark blue tunic and skirt.

One of the women who joined the WAPC was called Marjorie Sellek – interestingly the widow of Inspector Mark Sellek who was killed when Birmingham Police HQ took a direct hit during an air raid in April 1941, was also called Marjorie Sellek. We have been unable to confirm if this is the same person.

Digbeth Police Station had long since been used for training police officers from Birmingham and other forces around the country as there wasn't a national police training college at that time. The female auxiliary officers would also use these training facilities which consisted of a small rear yard for drill purposes and a gymnasium in the main building.

Women's Auxiliary Police marching in Digbeth Police Station's rear yard during the Second World War.

By comparison you can see little has changed at Digbeth Police Station since the war, from this picture showing how the women would look marching in the rear yard today.

Female members of the force undertaking self-defence training in Digbeth gym

Records of 146 Auxiliary Corps officers are held at the museum. 100 of them were in administrative roles prior to joining the police. They also include a former cook, a number of drivers, a handful who state their occupation as manageress, an ambulance driver and a member of the Women's Land Army.

115 of the women were single and at least two of them went on to marry serving police officers. Unlike the women police officers, the Auxiliary Corps were mainly local. A few originated from outside Birmingham – these include women born in Burma, Montreal and Ireland.

Most of the women were in their early 20s when they joined. A handful were between 18 and 20 and some were in their 30s, the oldest being 37.

The records show the maximum length of service was four years and two months. Only a few of the officers completed more than four years' service. 20 didn't complete a full year – two of those only did one month before their services were dispensed with! The reasons for leaving varied, including the following:

- 57 resigned
- 10 were 'released' (this might just be a difference in terminology for resigned – insufficient detail is held of the exact reasons for leaving in order to understand the difference)
- 39 left on medical grounds
- 22 show their 'services were dispensed with' by the Chief Constable
- 18 transferred to civilian staff following the disbanding of the Auxiliary Corps in March 1946

One transferee worthy of note is Marjorie Joan Lewis who completed a further 29 years' service as administrative staff in the Birmingham City Police.

Marjorie joined the WAPC in November 1941 and was promoted to leading auxiliary in June 1943. She became a civilian clerk upon transferring, before undertaking several years as an assistant staff officer and finally being promoted to senior clerk shortly before her retirement.

WAPC during gas mask training

The Chief Constable 'dispensing of the services' of auxiliaries was in relation to the Police (Employment & Offences) Order 1942. In November 1945 the Home Secretary decided to revoke the Police (Employment and Offences) Orders[141]. The conclusion of the Second World War meant that men were starting to return to the ranks of police forces and many auxiliary units were disbanded. Continuance of employment would be offered to suitable auxiliaries however whilst recruitment was ongoing to bring forces up to strength. This is reflected in the museum records as after this date all reasons for leaving are shown as 'resigned' or 'transfer to civilian staff'. Interestingly none of the Auxiliary Corps went on to become police officers in Birmingham.

Police Orders 29th March 1946 stated the Women's Auxiliary Police is to be disbanded and any remaining serving members will be retained in a clerical or other capacity as civilian employees. The Chief Constable wished to have his thanks to the department for their services during the war recorded, as they had in many instances replaced police officers for more active war duties in the Armed Forces.[142]

WAPC Ada Winifred Wesley, born in 1917, she joined in February 1943 and was previously a typist. She was from Birmingham and was based in Kenyon Street Police Station.

WAPC Jean Constance Mundy-Neill – aged 21, one of the few married officers in the WAPC. She was based on Moseley Street and was released after 9 months on medical grounds.

There are also records of three Wolverhampton Borough Women's Auxiliary Police Corps. It may be that more were recruited but their records have not survived, although it was a much smaller force with only two policewomen during the war so this may have been the complete establishment. They were 33, 25 and 31 years of age and two had previous occupations recorded (clerk and manageress). One was married and two were single, two of them worked in the Chief Constable's office and one worked in the Accident Department. Unlike the Birmingham City WAPC, two of the Wolverhampton women went on to become regular officers.

Birmingham Police Victory Parade, led by Women Police and WAPC

Colmore Row, Birmingham
World War II Victory Parade

1940s – Wartime and Beyond

Sergeant Evelyn Miles retired at the end of 1939 and thus a new era began for the Women Police in 1940. The breakdown for 1940 and 1941 is given by Inspector Doris Bushnell. It is split into additional categories and whilst the statistics are informative, the accompanying report giving context and further information about many of the categories is not given. Also missing is the rather personal summing up of the achievements and hard work of the female officers given in Sergeant Miles' reports.

The snapshot below shows some of the war time duties undertaken by the Women Police:

Summary of some of the Duties performed by
Women Police for 1940.

General enquiries made or dealt with	637.
Enquiries to trace relatives after bombing	100.
Enquiries made respecting missing persons.	66.
Enquiries at Hospitals re destitute persons etc.	9.
Alien enquiries.	76.
Military enquiries (Verify illness etc.)	65.
Do. Do. (circumstances of family)	32.
Do. Do. (Verification of bombing etc.)	41.
Billets found for members of the services.	19.

This section shows the number of hours patrolled each month in uniform and in plain clothes, with the total number in each at the far right:

												Total
uniform	289	239	177	215	195	168	146	187	206	262	259	659.	3242.
plain clothes	151	105	100	112	112	105	122	129	128	79	72	10	1225

Uniform patrol hours dipped in March and then during the summer between June and August. December clearly warranted much more uniformed patrol than plain clothes, clocking up more than three times the average hours of uniform patrol achieved during the previous 11 months!

This is the end of the detailed reports of the Women's Police Department held by the museum. Presumably further reports were made but these have not survived. Lots of information can still be gleaned about the role of the Women Police however from various different sources.

Early in 1940 a significant development was made with the deployment of policewomen when four of the officers were sent out to divisional stations, one of these being Agnes Tantrum. It would appear that the trial was successful as from the 1940s onwards, whilst still being managed centrally, female officers were posted to different divisions rather than all working out of the Women Police Department.

During 1941, the vice-president of the National Council of Women, Mrs Home Peel, was enquiring as to the current situation regarding police women across the country. The Coventry branch of the NCW wrote back to her to say that Coventry was in a very poor state of affairs following the Blitz with many people having left the city which had been so severely hit by air raids. She stated that three policewomen work for Coventry City Police but there are a further three vacancies that despite the force's best efforts, cannot be filled. She also indicates that the Chief Constable speaks very well of the women they do have and that one of them was commended for her bravery 'on the night of the Blitz'.[143]

The Chief Constable of Wolverhampton Borough Police wrote back to Mrs Peel to state that there were two regular attested policewomen in the force and the second one was appointed on the 22nd of January 1940.[144]

Birmingham Police Order of 1st December 1941 set out the specific occasions when plain clothes may be worn by police women:

- When required to accompany a CID officer on duties outside police premises
- When engaged on duties together with a plain clothed officer on division
- When employed on hospital observation
- When performing escort duties within or outside the city, other than where police transport is used

It also stated that it must be remembered that the Women Police Department is essentially a uniform branch of the police service, and that in more circumstances than not the wearing of police uniform will achieve the primary objects of efficient police duty in preference to plain clothes.

The Women Police Department continued their work with the girls' hostel which had been temporarily rehoused whilst the premises in Newton Street were used for police women's accommodation during the war. By 1945 new premises were sought for a hostel and after much haggling with the owner, 31 Aston Street was purchased. On 1st February 1946 the Salvation Army took over the administration of the work which changed its name to the Girls Night Shelter. In 1961 the Girls Night Shelter moved to 37 Portland Road, Edgbaston.

Police Orders from 1946 show the duties of women police were being discussed, with a view to them carrying out more detective work. It was stated that work being carried out by the police women on behalf of government departments would be reducing soon and they would therefore be free to carry out enquiries, leaving the detectives with more time to concentrate on the more serious crimes.[145]

Birmingham Policewomen c1940s

The personnel records show 47 female officers were recruited during the 1940s with an average age of 26. Surprisingly despite the recruitment freeze, records at the museum show that twenty-three women police officers were recruited during the war.

Only 15 of the women who joined in this decade were living in Birmingham at the time – the others came from all over the country, several from Scotland (one from Stornoway on the Isle of Lewis) and one from Ireland. All of them were single, including one widow. Nine of them went on to marry serving officers.

The women came from a wide variety of occupations. 27 came from clerical roles – typists, clerks and assistants. Seven were manual labourers such as farm hands. There were two nurses, two former auxiliary police officers from outside of Birmingham, a lead female firefighter, an optician, a school teacher and a sub-postmistress. Our personal favourite – a chicken hatchery assistant.

37 women left during the 1940s. Reasons vary as follows:

- Three to pursue a different career
- Five were dismissed (three deemed not likely to make efficient constables, one following a theft conviction and one following a disciplinary)
- Five for family reasons (mostly to care for sick parents)
- Three due to ill-health (two of these were ill-health retirements)
- 11 to get married
- Two retired
- Three transferred out (Kent, Carmarthenshire and Taunton being the lucky recipients of exports of the Birmingham City Police)
- Four were unhappy with the job
- One left after struggling with the balance of work and home responsibilities

The average length of a police career for women who joined in the 1940s was six years and 10 months (calculated from the records held in the museum). This doesn't give credit to the lengthy careers of women like Helen Beattie – who retired after 30 years at the rank of chief inspector, or Catherine Bruce who retired after 28 at the rank of sergeant.

By the start of 1949 the number of women police had increased to 27, but one inspector post had been lost. By the end of 1949 the authorised establishment had risen to 35 with posts for one chief inspector, two inspectors, four sergeants and 28 policewomen constables. The work of the Women Police Department expanded throughout 1949 and female constables were attached to the woman detective sergeant for training in CID. By now the women police were becoming more involved in specialist roles and attending additional training courses such as the CID course in Wakefield Detective Training Centre. Policewoman Helen Beattie attended this course in West Riding in the summer of 1946 – she scored 91% in the final examination and came top in the class of 16 students.

Sergeant Florrie Schipper (left) and the Women Police

Removal of the marriage ban & other key developments

In 1946, in a massive breakthrough for equality for female officers, the ban on employing married women was lifted and the requirement for a woman to resign on marriage was removed.[146]

Maternity rights (or lack thereof as could be considered in the context of today's equality and diversity legislation!) were also stated in the Police (Women) Regulations Amendments of 1946. These being:

- A maternity period is 6 months before the estimated date of birth and 9 months after it
- A married policewoman will not be entitled to sick leave for any injury or illness solely related to pregnancy, childbirth or their aftereffects *(interesting – what about unmarried policewomen who are pregnant?)*
- Maternity leave may be granted for the whole or any part of the maternity period
- Paid maternity leave is 3 months, will not be granted until probation is completed and no more than 3 months paid maternity leave can be taken in any 12 month period
- A claim cannot be made for medical care or dental treatment during unpaid maternity leave
- Unpaid maternity leave will not be taken into account when calculating the service of a policewoman

In 1948, female officers were allowed to join the Police Federation and the term 'police officer' (rather than policeman or policewoman) was recognised by the Home Office.

TANTRUM : Agnes May,

Agnes May Tantrum was born on 16th June 1897 in Bucknall, Shropshire. She joined Birmingham City Police on 17th April 1931 after previously being employed as a pattern card worker.

She was promoted to sergeant in 1941 and inspector in 1954, becoming an acting chief inspector on the 1st April 1957. In an interview with the Birmingham Mail when she retired, she stated she had thoroughly enjoyed her career as a policewoman and if she could have her time again, she would do the same job[147].

In 1940 she was one of the first four policewomen sent out to work from a divisional station. In 1952, as a sergeant approaching 55 years of age she asked that the relevant pension regulations be waived to allow her to continue serving in the force and qualify for a pension. Agnes Tantrum was one of five women chosen to represent Birmingham Police at the Royal Review of Police at Hyde Park in 1954.

Sergeant Tantrum on the right

She reluctantly retired as she had reached the compulsory retirement age of 60 in 1957. In a report by Superintendent Norah Gray after she submitted her intention to retire, it was stated:

'She has taken a very active part in training recruits and in building up the Policewomen Department to its present strength and scope. Because of this, I shall always regard her as a Birmingham pioneer whose zeal, enthusiasm and example had great influence on the entrants to the Policewomen's Department in Birmingham. I consider that her contribution to the Policewomen's Service has been of the greatest value and shall be most sorry when she must sever her connection with the Department.'[148]

She died in 1984 aged 86.

Ivy Dugard was born in 1908 in Birmingham. She had twin older siblings, a brother and sister who were four years older than her. Another earlier brother had died at three years old before Ivy and her other siblings were born. She applied to join the Birmingham Women Police in May 1932 but was told there were no vacancies and she would be put on the waiting list. By October 1932 she wrote again, telling how she had been following the work of the women police and she was 'keener than ever!'

The officer who made enquiries as to her suitability reported her to be 'well-spoken, and seems very straightforward and direct in her manner, and imbued with plenty of common sense.' As was common practice at the time he enquired as to whether Ivy or anyone in her family had ever suffered from epilepsy or lunacy and reported back that they had not. He also stated that she had good knowledge of first aid, had regularly helped out with street accidents and had subsequently accompanied the police to hospital several times, 'she not being at all nervous on these occasions'.

She was eventually able to join the force in January 1934. She completed several successful years with the force before she started to suffer with stomach pains in January 1942. On the 24th January the force doctor was called and sent her immediately to hospital. She was operated on for an acute intestinal obstruction but the surgeons noticed 'miliary tubercles' on her intestines. She was reported to be suffering with 'consumptive bowels' and her case was reported to the 'TB Authorities'. Tuberculosis was a huge problem in the UK during the early part of the 20th Century, with a vaccine not being developed until the 1950s. It was not uncommon for the force to lose several officers a year from this illness.

Ivy left the force in 1942 on account of her forthcoming marriage to PC C326 Patrick Dixon. She was asked if she wished to stay on as a Police War Reserve Constable but she stated she did not wish to lose her present status as a police woman and go to a lower scale of pay. Inspector Bushnell told her she would therefore unfortunately have to resign on marriage. She died in January 1952.

Alice Norah Rigby Turner was born in Grimsby in 1902. In her letter of interest to the Chief Constable in 1935, she stated she was short listed to join the Metropolitan Police. She had carried out administrative work for the previous 12 years but stated she had always been interested in police work.

She was added to the waiting list and joined the force in January 1936. In April 1943 an incident involving Miss Turner was reported when Police Woman Sergeant Ross witnessed her pushing her bicycle towards the station cat (who had recently been recruited to help rid the station of mice) and allegedly hit the cat hard on the bottom. Sergeant Ross stated Miss Turner had a reputation for hurting cats and so she gave her a hard push on the side of the head. The first event with the bicycle was witnessed by Police Woman Sergeant Tantrum but she did not see the second.

The matter was reported and the Assistant Chief Constable Edward Dodd saw both women in his office at which point he told Miss Turner 'she had acted in a manner most unbecoming for a woman of her age and particularly inconsistent with the conduct of a woman police officer'. She had requested a full enquiry into the matter but was told this would not take place as it was not deemed necessary to waste further police time or paper on this incident. Sergeant Ross was told not to repeat her action. Miss Bushnell had informed the Assistant

Chief Constable that Miss Turner's service had been most unsatisfactory recently.

By May 1943 the women police were working closely with the Auxiliary Territorial Service (the Women's branch of the Army during the Second World War) to locate absentee ATS members and by all accounts were working very well together, with one exception. All the members of the ATS had complained about one officer in particular – Miss Turner. They described her as a 'grouser who has turned sour on her job' and stated she did more than her fair share of grumbling. This came to a head during one evening when a member of the ATS reported that Miss Turner had carried out a very half-hearted tour of duty, not checking all the places they were supposed to patrol and not following through on reports because she couldn't be bothered. It was reported that back in the station when Miss Turner was offered a seat in the chair belonging to Miss Bushnell, she replied 'I don't want to get scabies, foot and mouth disease or Miss Bushnell-itis'. The corporal reported the matter as she took offence although she was reassured by Policewoman Richardson that the comment was not directed at her, but was in relation to the homeless children who sometimes sat in it when they were brought into the office. Miss Turner was subsequently found guilty of disciplinary offences (neglect of duty, disobedience of orders and discreditable conduct – in that she acted in a manner likely to bring discredit upon the reputation of the force) and required to resign from the force.

Miss Turner consequently became the second member of the Women Police to be required to leave following a disciplinary hearing.

First Birmingham Female Special Constables

The Special Constabulary have been a great asset to police forces across Britain for many years. Their numbers swelled greatly during both World Wars as regular officers joined the armed forces but there is little information on female special constables. Having researched the registers of Birmingham special constables since World War 1 it is not until the 6th December 1949 that we find the first entries relating to female special constables. Finally after years of inequality and discrimination 12 women joined the ranks on this date:

Name	Age	Occupation	Divisional number
Margaret Delaney	38 yrs	Shorthand typist	W1
Joyce Clarke	29yrs	Shorthand typist	W2
Marjorie Lewis	31yrs	Shorthand typist	W3
Bessie Thomas	33yrs	Shorthand typist	W4
Jean Varley	26yrs	Shorthand typist	W5
Marjorie Begett	36yrs	Secretary	W6
Betty Chamberlain	28yrs	Shorthand typist	W7
Lilian Haddock	32yrs	Shorthand typist	W8
Hilda Gidney	28yrs	Shorthand typist	W9
Hilda Hammond	38yrs	u/k	W10
Vera Haill	29yrs	Clerk typist	W11
Marie Lea	31yrs	Shorthand typist	W12

It is interesting to note that nearly all of the new officers have a clerical background but a reason for this is not given. They were however posted on various divisions throughout the force.

1950s: Post-war & Urbanisation

By December 1950 the establishment strength of Birmingham City Police was 2,058 men and 35 women (the women had never achieved full strength at this number). The actual strength was 1,522 men and 33 woman – making just over 2% of the workforce female. By the end of the decade in 1959 there were 160 more male constables and 32 women on the strength – now less than 2% of officers were female. Attraction and retention of suitable candidates proved difficult, but this was also a problem for the recruitment of male officers during this time period. The Chief Constable had taken to writing to other forces to ask for details of candidates they had turned down in order to identify men to recruit as constables![149]

One of the great innovations of the 1950s was the introduction of police dogs. On the 9th July 1951 PC Ford and his dog Flash took to the streets of Birmingham. It would be another 29 years before the West Midlands had its first female dog handler.

Birmingham became the first provincial borough force to have a Chief Inspector of Women Police when Norah Gray was promoted on the 1st of January 1950. In an article commemorating the occasion in the Birmingham Mail, Chief Constable Edward Dodd stated:[150]

'Policewomen in Birmingham have been accepted as an integral part of the force for a very long time, and I am completely satisfied that they fulfil a very real need for police work. There are many types of enquiry that they perform equally well, if not better than men… I only wish that a greater number of suitable women would come forward to make the Police Service their career'.

The force re-organised into 6 divisions in 1952 and female officers were aligned to these as follows:

A division 232 male officers 0 female
B division 159 male officers 2 female
C division 251 male officers 4 female
D division 230 male officers 4 female
E Division 202 male officers 4 female
F Division 238 male officers 4 female

Some were attached to the Criminal Investigation Department and other specialist departments, and several remained in the Women Police Department. Many of the women police undertook traffic control duties such as the officer in this picture:

The need for accommodation for policewomen was a pressing one at this time and the Watch Committee subsequently purchased a large house at 106 Anderton Road, Moseley, known as Burgess House. This had previously been a nurses' hostel and was converted into single quarters for nine policewomen and a housekeeper. This was followed in 1954 by the purchasing of 108 Anderton Road for additional accommodation. A further premises on Anderton Road (no. 97) was also used to house eight/nine policewomen. Burgess house remained in police possession for many years and during this time was known by several other names - the most respectable being the 'convent'.

For once, the different rules for policewomen worked in their favour in 1959 when the Birmingham Watch Committee were informed that constables had requested permission to patrol in shirt sleeve order by removing their tunics. The largest voice against this was from the Police Federation who argued that the officers were issued with a lightweight summer uniform anyway. But let us remember that the policewomen were allowed to remove their police tunics whilst on patrol.[151]

Policewomen in Birmingham – Sergeant Agnes Hornick is on the right

Records are held in the police museum for 139 women who joined during the 1950s – almost three times as many as in the 1940s and more than seven times as many as in the 1930s. The average age was 23 and the first teenager was employed in 1953 – 18-year-old Eunice

Priddey. She left in 1957 after marrying another officer and struggling to get a work/life balance.

The majority of women recruited now came from the local area – 95 were from Birmingham and a further six from the West Midlands area. Outside of the Midlands one was born in Malaya and one Rhodesia. Also for the first time, more women came to Birmingham City Police from Ireland and Wales than Scotland.

Although the marriage ban for female recruits was lifted in 1946 – the files at the museum show that only one of the women recruited during the 1950s was married. She was actually a transferee from Lincolnshire and already married to another officer. A further 56 of the women went on to marry officers from West Midlands and other forces around the country. Some were from local forces but others were from far away forces where officers had met on training courses. The vast majority of these women left the police service following their marriage, birth of their first child or after struggling to maintain an effective work/life balance.

Quoted from the file of one female officer who joined in the 1950s but then resigned after eight months in order to marry an officer from Staffordshire County Police before completing her probationary period:

"She assured us at interview she had no plans to marry. This appears to be another training school romance."

From the records held by the museum we can tell that the average length of a career was four years and three months. This needs to be considered with the caveat that seven of the 139 records are not complete and the end date and therefore length of service for those seven women has not been recorded and could not be factored in to the average. It is likely these women had longer careers and that is why their full records are not at the museum. There may also be other women from this time period who completed in excess of 20 years' service whose records are still held corporately and are therefore unavailable to the museum.

Only one file for a woman who joined during the 1950s and reached 30 years' service is held with the museum records. Sergeant Edith Mary Smith joined in 1957 aged 26. She is recorded as retiring 30 years later in 1987, having reached the 'compulsory retirement age for her rank.'

100 of the women came from administrative roles. Five of the women transferred in from other police forces and one had previous experience as a Birmingham City Police woman. Several professional occupations are listed again including radiographer, registrar and school teacher. Other occupations including ambulance driver, Women's RAF, nursery nurse and milk tester are also listed. Some of the women came from various manual labour roles with occupations such as agricultural worker, gardener and farm hand being recorded.

The reasons for leaving during the 1950s have been broken down as follows:

- One couldn't settle in Birmingham
- 16 left for different careers
- Two were dismissed following disciplinary procedures
- One was dismissed after it was determined she was unlikely to make an efficient constable
- Three emigrated (two to join husbands in police roles in Nairobi and Malaya, one to join Rhodesia Police)
- Six left for family reasons (mainly to look after sick parents)
- Eight left through ill-health
- 35 left to get married

- Five left following a pregnancy
- Three left following relationship difficulties
- One resigned before being dismissed (pregnant and unmarried)
- Two retired
- Two transferred to other forces (Walsall and West Riding)
- 10 left after struggling to find a work/life balance
- One female officer died

LAW: Jeanie Sarah Stirling

Jeanie Sarah Stirling Law was born in Lanark, a small town in the central belt of Scotland on 21st January 1916. She joined Birmingham City Police on 13th October 1941. She was a qualified optician and had been a member of the local Voluntary Aid Detachment of the Red Cross for four years. She was very involved in her local community and her references include a testimonial from the reverend of her local church who stated she had been actively associated with church work, particularly with regards to young people, for the previous 10 years.

She stated in her application that she left school young due to circumstances at home, however she covered any lost ground in evening classes.

Once appointed she was required to live at a local hostel (men would have been required to live in Single Men's Quarters, normally attached to police stations).

Miss Law was made of strong stuff – on 11th March 1941 in a report to her superintendent, she stated she was bitten by a mongrel dog on her leg on the 9th March. She attended hospital along with Sergeant Tantrum where the wound was cauterised and she received an anti-tetanus injection. She then resumed her duty immediately.[152]

She was highly commended twice during the 1940s for her work in connection with raids on brothels and betting houses.

She was promoted to sergeant in 1947 after coming top of her class during the promotion exams.

Jeanie was promoted to temporary inspector on 1st January 1950 and became substantive in this rank on 3rd January 1951. She was promoted to chief inspector in November 1954.

She transferred to West Riding in 1957 to be their first female superintendent, one of only a handful of women employed at this rank across the country. She later became an Assistant Inspector of Constabulary in 1962 and Birmingham Chief Constable Edward Dodd wrote to her to congratulate her and stated 'we shall look forward to our first inspection!!'[153]

Women police hockey teams around the country now compete every year to win the Jean Law Trophy (the national Police Sport UK Ladies Hockey trophy) which the West Midlands Police team has won on several occasions during the 1980s and 1990s.

This photo was taken in May 1998 to celebrate West Midlands Police beating the Metropolitan Police team to win the trophy:

Back row left to right: Deb Menzel, Barbara Langford, Nicola Court, Jayne Roberts, Liz Camfield, Jan Needham, Helen Kirkman. Front row left to right: Megan Heather-Shaw, Lynne Harrison, Chief Constable Edward Crew, Jo Smallwood and Hayley Brewster.

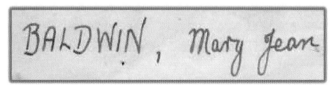

Mary Jean Baldwin was born in 1925 in Preston. She joined Birmingham City Police on 3rd December 1949.

In May 1954 Mary was sent on a 10 week CID course. As an aid attached to the Criminal Investigation Department she was paid a plain clothes allowance, detective duty and detectives duty allowance. The question arose as to what allowances she was entitled to whilst on the course as it was the first instance of a policewoman aid being sent on a course of this nature.

She was promoted to sergeant in 1955 and passed the relevant exams for promotion to inspector by 1957. In recommending her for an instructor's course in 1955, Superintendent Norah Gray describes her as a woman of sterling character. Due to Sergeant Baldwin's late application, the Chief Constable ended up writing to the Police College asking for her to take the place of the candidate he had previously nominated – Police Woman Wren (who later became Chief Superintendent Wren!).

In March 1958 Mary applied for an inspector position in the Cheshire Constabulary. In the supporting letter from Norah Gray she is described as being 'well qualified with the desirable characteristics' with natural 'buoyancy of spirit'. Miss Gray stated she would be well suited to the work of a rural officer but indicates she would be sorry to see her leave Birmingham.

On the 8th June 1959 Sergeant Baldwin was engaged on enquiries at Selly Oak hospital taking a statement. After she had finished her enquiries she was going back down the stairs when she slipped and fell, fracturing her ankle. She was signed off work accordingly and tragically died on the 26th June 1959. During the inquest her cause of death was recorded as a pulmonary embolism – a blood clot that moved from the vicinity of the injury to a pulmonary artery. It is associated with inactivity following an injury and this cause of death was recorded as being common, but unusual in a person of Sergeant Baldwin's age (34).

Her story was recently uncovered whilst digitising the files held at the museum and her name has been added to the West Midlands Police Roll of Honour. She is recorded as the first female officer to die on duty, or through an injury received whilst on duty, in West Midlands Police or any of its predecessor forces.

Florence Schipper was born in November 1907 and originated from Stafford. She joined Birmingham City Police in March 1933 having previously been a shop assistant.

She was complimented in February 1942 for good work in connection with brothels, a betting house and a gaming house.

Florence became interested in darts during the early part of the Second World War. Policewomen were used in fire watching, even when there were

no air raids expected. During these long, dull hours Florence helped pass the time by playing darts.

Remembering this time, Florence said: "In the early part of the war the men nearly always won any darts match which I was playing against them – I always got my leg pulled!"

Florence got better at the game however, and went on to win the All England Policewoman's Darts Championships held in Preston in 1952. She beat off stiff competition from a Norwich policewoman, beating her two games to one.

After her victory she was quoted as saying: "Now I've learnt to play and I'm winning, the men don't like taking me on! [154]

She was promoted to sergeant in 1945 and retired after 30 years' service in 1963.

Retired PW Florrie Schipper

1960s – Evolution, Political Development and Amalgamations

In the early 1960s the work of the Women Police Department remained largely the same. They were responsible for the control of traffic and road crossings together with taking statements. They also had responsibility for work in relation to young girls and sexual offences. The establishment in 1960 stood at 107 female officer but the actual number was only 69 due to difficulties in recruiting and retaining suitable female officers.

By this time the Women Police Department had its own superintendent and posts for one chief inspector, three inspectors, 14 sergeants and 88 women constables. What a contrast to 1917 when there were just two officers who were making the adjustment from lock-up matron to patrolling the streets of Birmingham.

The shortage of officers continued and in 1961 the Chief Constable was moved to write 'I am convinced that much greater use could be made of the services of police women if they were available in sufficient number.' By 1965 the establishment had increased to 145 although in reality there were only 105 women.

In 1961 another key development came in the fight for equal rights and representation for female police officers, when the Police Federation Act 1961 gave Women Police full representative and voting rights.

It is now that the work of the women police really started to evolve significantly and it was the late 1960s where real progress was made to bring the Women Police into line with the roles and responsibilities of their male colleagues. In 1965 policewomen had branched out into other policing areas such as working in the information room and accident enquiry teams and eventually walking the beats. The 1966 re-organisation of the Women Police Department also paved the way for further integration with the rest of the force, with more police women being posted to divisions under the supervision of the divisional chief superintendent.

153 officers are showing in the museum's records as joining in the 1960s. Two were married and one was a widow. 80 were from Birmingham and 73 were from different parts of the country and abroad. One was born in India and in this decade more came from Ireland than Scotland or Wales.

Only 58 came from administrative roles, with eight having previous experience as a police officer. One came from the Women's RAF, one was a prison officer and one a firewoman.

Six of the records for women who joined in the 1960s are incomplete and we cannot calculate their length of service. For the remaining 147 women, the average length of career three years eight months.

Of the 156 women who left in the 1960s, reasons for leaving have been identified for the following:

- 44 wanted a change in career
- One was dismissed following a conviction
- Three emigrated and two moved within the UK
- Four left for family reasons
- Five left for reasons of ill-health (all young in service – the longest being three years & five months)
- One was injured on duty and did not wish to spend her two to three year recovery period working as a restricted officer
- 30 left to get married
- 33 left after becoming pregnant or following the birth of a child
- One left because of a relationship
- Three retired
- One returned to her home country (Canada)
- 10 transferred out
- One left because of issues travelling to work
- Five left to go travelling abroad

- 11 were struggling to combine their work with household duties

Significantly more women were leaving because they were dissatisfied with police work or wanted a change of career – by now this had taken over as the number one reason for women leaving Birmingham City Police. Whereas over a third of women left to get married in the 1950s, less than a fifth of female officers left for this reason in the 1960s. The amount leaving following a pregnancy went up considerably - over a fifth of women leaving for this reason compared to only 5% in the 1950s. This demonstrates that more women were staying following a marriage and then later deciding to leave when starting a family.

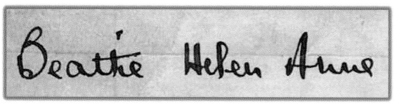

Helen Anne Beattie was born in Cabrach, Scotland on 26th August 1911 and joined the Birmingham City Police in October 1941 when she was

living in Aderdeen.

She spent a large part of her career in the CID, after becoming one of the first female officers from Birmingham to be sent on the detective training course conducted by West Riding Constabulary in the summer of 1946. She came first place in a class of 16 with 91% in the final examination. Later that year she became a temporary sergeant after passing her promotion exams.

In 1948 as a sergeant she was

recommended along with a few other officers to be sent on a Police College course, completing Course A successfully and returning in 1962 to complete Course B.

Whilst within the CID she was involved in all aspects of major crime investigation including murder, infanticide, abortion, bigamy, perjury and larceny and was commended twice for her work in cases of illegal abortions and once for raids carried out on brothels and betting houses.

From January 1950 she was promoted to inspector and was responsible for training policewomen in detective work and supervising the detective policewomen attached to Detective Departments on divisions.

Chief Inspector Helen Beattie – far left

Between 1958 and 1960 Miss Beattie was the Women Inspector's representative on the Police Federation Joint Branch Board and always took an interest in the welfare and efficiency of policewomen through the board.

At the start of 1960 she was promoted to chief inspector and went back into uniform. Superintendent Norah Gray wrote after six months that the promotion has been one that the department has benefited from and that Miss

Beattie was highly competent, conscientious, kind and sympathetic and she felt she was very happy to be working in the Women Police Department.

In 1971 she reached the upper age limit for her rank of 60, seven weeks before she was due to retire after 30 years' service. She applied to be able to complete the seven weeks and this was approved.

She subsequently retired on superannuation on 12th October 1971 with her certificate of service marked exemplary. She died in August 1988.

CROCKER, Kathleen Edith Eileen.

Kathleen Edith Eileen Crocker was born on 31st October 1922 in Wales. Her father was a policeman and she first applied in 1941, whilst living in Birmingham, but was under the minimum age for new recruits and advised to consider becoming a member of the Women's Auxiliary Police Corps instead. It would seem this did not appeal as she applied again in 1943 and in 1944 shortly before she turned 22 to see if she could now apply.

Kathleen eventually joined Birmingham City Police on 13th November 1944 and served until the 6th March 1950 when she transferred to Cardiff.

She was attached to the CID for three months in 1948 – her duties involved taking statements for offences such as infanticide, abortion, bigamy, forgery, false pretences and larceny. The only fault the department found with her was that she could be a little 'strong-willed'. Clearly not a quality sought after in policewomen in the 1940s!

She transferred to Cardiff in 1950, a force which had only recently appointed women police in the 1940s, as she felt there would be more opportunities there for her. Just over four months later in July 1950 she had resigned for personal reasons and moved back to Birmingham. She stated in a letter to the Chief Constable that she understood the Chief of Cardiff spoke to him at a conference and told him she had left Cardiff and why, and that he was willing to accept her back into the Birmingham force. She promptly re-joined.

During her service she was complimented four times and highly commended once. She was promoted to the rank of sergeant in August 1952.

By 1958 she was applying for inspector positions in other forces - in 1959 she turned down a post at Eastbourne Police due to a housing shortage and not being able to find a house or flat for her and her mother. In October 1961 she was appointed an inspector in the Newcastle-upon-Tyne City Police.

It wasn't long before she returned to the West Midlands - becoming Walsall's first female inspector on the 1st of April 1963.

It was reported in the Sunday Mercury that:

'A room at Walsall Police Station has been newly decked out in primrose and blue paint, gay multi-coloured curtains, fitted carpet and brand new office furniture. The whole interior exudes femininity into a building which is so much a man's world. In fact the room has been decorated as part of a welcome to a member of the fairer sex - the Borough's first woman police-inspector. Miss Kathleen Crocker has arrived at Walsall to head the Division's team of 11 police-women, one woman police-sergeant and two girl cadets.'[155]

In the accompanying interview Miss Crocker stated 'most women leave the police force for marriage, and not because they dislike the work. For those who stay on after marriage, there are not many concessions but if the husband happens to be a member of the force then care is taken to ensure that days off and annual leave coincide'.

It is sad to think that almost 20 years after the marriage ban being lifted, most women still felt the need to leave the police upon marriage. However we were still a long way away from the flexibility that exists today to help officers achieve a good work/life balance.

LANGFORD, Joan

One officer worthy of mention at this point is Police Woman Joan Langford. She joined Birmingham City Police in 1946, leaving in 1957 to set up her own business but returning in 1958.

A lovely article appeared in the Birmingham Mail in 1957[156] where she recollected some of her stories of policing in Birmingham. One story relates to an off-duty arrest she had to make whilst on her way home one night when she came across a man lying in the gutter on Colmore

Row. Upon closer inspection she realised he was drunk and could not be left there. She managed to haul him to his feet and drag him into the nearest phone box where she called the police for assistance. Upon hearing the word 'police' the man started and struggled free – running off into St. Philip's Churchyard. Not wanting to be left waiting with no prisoner when help arrived she took chase. After he fell down, Miss Langford could not get him back up again. She started dragging him by the collar whilst he was on all fours, making steady progress back through the churchyard! An old lady saw them and assessed the situation, subsequently giving advice that she should sit him on the bench for a few minutes. Miss Langford replied 'Thanks very much, but he will be all right where I am taking him'! She eventually got her prisoner to the lock-up at Steelhouse Lane and the magistrate was incredulous when she appeared with her prisoner at court the following day upon hearing that she brought him in alone.

Miss Langford was commended on 12 occasions during her career for her efforts in bringing offenders to justice and for good police work.

In 1965 she suffered an injury whilst on her way home from duty – she called at the house of another police woman to inform her of a change to her tour of duty. She suffered a severe fracture to her lower leg and after many complications in 1966 it was decided that the best medical course of action was to amputate her lower left leg. This operation took place in 1966 and after some initial nervousness Miss Langford returned to work. She was very concerned about how she would look in uniform with her artificial limb and was worried about what colleagues and members of the public would think, but this worry eased and she settled back in well.

Unfortunately she experienced further health problems throughout the rest of the 1960s, leading to several operations to remove cysts.

After being very sick for most of 1970 she eventually died in October 1970 aged 52.

Pauline Elsie Wren, born 22nd July 1926, joined Birmingham City Police on the 11th April 1950. She was promoted to sergeant in 1955 and inspector in 1959.

In May 1955 she was highly commended for action she took at the Sutton Coldfield railway disaster.

From May 1957 to August 1958 she was seconded to the British Police Unit in Cyprus. In August 1960 she transferred to Leeds City Police where she attained the rank of chief inspector, before returning to Birmingham in 1966 as a superintendent.

A report from her file dated 25th June 1966 shows she attended a Senior Staff Course at the Police College whilst in the rank of superintendent in Leeds City Police. The report gives a glowing account of her performance and conduct on the course:

'Women Superintendent Wren is a very shrewd and sensible officer. Her disarming personality conceals considerable determination and self-confidence. She is kindly, thoughtful and her genuineness and sincerity have ensured her being well liked by all her colleagues on the Senior Staff Course.

She made great and commendable efforts to be on equal terms with her male fellow students, working very hard indeed, and succeeded in this with notable good humour. A very capable debater, she was understandably inclined to do battle in the policewomen's cause but she was always ready to put forward ideas on all aspects and branches of the Service. She was fearless in argument and her high intelligence and wide experience enabled her to stand up to any opposition.

Women Superintendent Wren is devoted to the Service. During her College training it has been evident that she has qualities that fit her for the highest posts open to women police officers.'

In 1971 she was promoted to temporary chief superintendent before she gained the substantive rank in 1974, becoming the West Midlands' first female chief superintendent.

She retired on the 30th April 1980, completing just over 30 years' service.

Barbara Mary Denis de Vitré

Whilst Miss de Vitré did not work for a police service in the West Midlands, her work will certainly have affected the role of women police in Birmingham and the wider West Midlands, directly and indirectly, and it would be wrong to have a book about the development of the role of women in the police service without mentioning her.

We have already seen how Norah Gray applied for the position of staff officer at HMIC which was vacated by Miss de Vitré when she became the first female Assistant Inspector of Constabulary (a role later carried out by Miss Jeanie Law) and she chaired the committee who chose the women police to be seconded to Cyprus (Pauline Wren among them).

She served with HMIC from 1945 to 1960 and during this time the number of police women rose from 445 to over 2500. Her prediction in 1929, that 'in 20 years' time the policewoman will be looked on as an essential factor of our social life, and the world will be amazed that such a natural reform could ever have been the subject of such bitter altercation'[157] could certainly be seen as being fulfilled.

Miss de Vitré initially joined the Women's Auxiliary Police Service after finding out about them on a social welfare training course and she went on to join Sheffield Constabulary in 1928.

In 1931 she became the head female constable in Cairo City Police with the task of setting up a branch of Egyptian women police.

She left in 1932 and in 1933 joined Leicester Constabulary. Here she was responsible for work on illegal abortion and once posed undercover as a heavily pregnant woman to secure arrest of abortionist.

She organised the first ever UK policewoman's conference in March 1937, which due to the onset of war, was not repeated until 1947, where she ended up being a speaker. In 1944 she became an inspector in the Kent County Constabulary where she organised a women's branch.

She successfully applied for the first role in Government specifically to look at the role of women police which was set up by Home Secretary

Herbert Morrison in 1944. She beat others to the role of HMIC 'Staff Officer' which involved assisting inspectors, chief police officers and police authorities on all issues surrounding police women and auxiliaries. In this position she had to convince many Chief Constables who were against the concept of women police and did not understand the value they could bring.

Miss de Vitré was appointed Assistant Inspector of Constabulary from May 1948. She needed a staff officer herself later - Kathleen Hill from the Metropolitan Police beat Norah Gray to this position. In 1951 she came to the Midlands to inspect the Dudley women police.

Later accolades include advising the US on public safety in their zone of post-war Germany in 1949, receiving the OBE in the 1951 birthday honours list and in 1957 she chaired a selection board deciding on a suitable contingent of policewomen to send to Cyprus. Women were given an upgrading of rank, a gratuity for every three months they remained, issued with a uniform and given free living quarters on these 12 month secondments.

She was also a special guest of the Irish police in 1959 helping to select their first batch of women police. She died after a battle with cancer in 1960.[158]

1960s amalgamations

Following the recommendations of the 1960 Royal Commission on the Police, Dudley Borough Police was merged with Walsall Borough Police, Wolverhampton Borough Police, parts of the Staffordshire

Constabulary and parts of the Worcestershire Constabulary, to become the West Midlands Constabulary from 1 April 1966.[159]

In 1966 the Home Secretary announced further amalgamations that would see Coventry City Police merged with Warwickshire to become Warwickshire and Coventry Constabulary in 1969.

West Midlands Constabulary

The West Midlands Constabulary (or West Midlands Police Force as it was often referred to) existed from April 1966 to April 1974 – a total of eight years. It covered the five boroughs of Walsall, Warley, West Bromwich, Wolverhampton and Dudley.

The first Chief Constable was Norman W. Goodchild (former Chief of Wolverhampton Borough Police) who held the post for the first year. He was succeeded by Edwin Solomon (former Chief of Walsall Borough Police) who remained in post until the force was amalgamated into the West Midlands Police in 1974.

The West Midlands Constabulary had a Women Police Department which existed right through the life of the force. Similar to the set up in Birmingham City, some of the women were posted out to divisions and specialist departments, although there appears to have been a lot of frustration at the limitations placed on female officers.

Excluding the three officers who came from Wolverhampton (as their figures are included in the Wolverhampton officers section), the average length of career for the 81 female officers in the West Midlands Constabulary whose files are held by the museum is just short of three years. This is slightly misleading as there will have been some officers who remained well into the introduction of West Midlands Police whose files are still considered 'live' and therefore not held by the museum, but this will have been a relatively small number, as the majority of women were still leaving the police service during this time period after getting married or becoming pregnant.

43 (over 50%) were cadets. Former occupations for the others include clerks, typists, nursing roles, shop and laboratory assistants, a machine operator, a hairdresser and a nanny. Several had former law and order roles – with five policewomen, a member of the Women's Auxiliary Air Force, a member of the Women's Royal Air Force and a member of the Women's Land Army.

76 of the women were single, three married and two divorced when they joined. 13 of the women married fellow officers during their service.

70 of the women resigned, one left on pension and one was medically unfit. Eight women transferred out – three to neighbouring Staffordshire County, one to Derbyshire, two to Dorset, one to Devon and one to Hampshire. Of the women who resigned:

- 15 left because they were unhappy
- 12 left following a marriage or due to a relationship
- Eight had gained alternative employment
- Five left for personal reasons
- Five left after becoming pregnant
- Two struggled to leave a work/life balance
- One emigrated
- One was allowed to resign following multiple disciplinaries
- One left for family reasons
- One left for medical reasons

By 1969 a chief superintendent from the E division noticed the difficulties in retaining married female officers, particularly when they were married to a fellow officer. He asked one female officer if she would consider withdrawing her resignation if her shifts could be brought more into line with her husbands, to which she said yes. He pointed out the difficulties in arranging for the married officers to work less late shifts and how challenging that would make it for the remaining female officers. In a report to the Chief Constable, he proposed a system whereby female officers could choose to work a shift system which meant only a third of their shifts were late shifts, rather than half. He had canvassed views of female officers and with half of them wanting the old system and half of them liking the suggested system, he felt this could function successfully as a combined system. He stated:

```
'I understand in the past there has been a refusal
to allow the Policewomen, on occasion, to change
shifts one for another. Provided this is only done
occasionally, I recommend it be allowed. In
addition, Sir, in the case of this Policewoman, and
in any other case of a Policewoman being married to
a Police Officer, you may feel prepared to allow
them to (where so desired) take the same additional
rest days off as their husbands.'
```

Very few records are held of women from the West Midlands Constabulary who attained the rank of sergeant and above. One of those women is Evelyn Unett.

Evelyn Mary Unett

Evelyn Maston was born on the 10th July 1929 and joined Staffordshire County Police on the 30th July 1949. She spent most of her career working in Brierley Hill. In 1954 she got married and became Evelyn Unett.

Evelyn was commended on multiple occasions throughout her career including:

- In 1960 commended by Chief Constable for work in CID leading to the arrest and conviction of a man for making indecent phone calls.
- In 1964 commended by Chief Constable following the conviction of a women for 32 offences of stealing in Stafford

In November 1965 she was admitted as a Serving Sister in The Order of St John of Jerusalem.

With the introduction of the West Midlands Constabulary, Evelyn became a superintendent, transferring from Staffordshire to the new force along with many other officers.

Evelyn was head of the Women Police Department in the constabulary until the amalgamation in 1974 which led to the West Midlands Police. After subsequently working in the Complaints Department for several years, in 1978 she was promoted to chief superintendent. This made her the first married female officer to achieve this rank in the West Midlands.

She retired from the force in October 1982 after completing over 33 years' service.

Improvements to equipment

1960s saw the introduction of the first panda cars – three Austin A40s were received at Belgrave Road Police Station in 1966 in a pilot scheme that was rolled out in 1967.

This decade also saw the arrival of two-way radios in 1966 with the Pye two handset pocket radios.

Police Cadets

The 1960s saw the introduction of female police cadets with records held at the museum of 84 female cadets from Birmingham, eight from Walsall, five from Wolverhampton and 45 from the West Midlands Constabulary.

The Birmingham cadets had originally been formed in 1949 and provided a steady flow of young blood into the organisation. In the 1950s they were seen as one of the major contributors to recruitment and the backbone of Birmingham City Police. In 1960 the establishment of the Cadet Corps stood at 101 male and for the first time 10 females. The pay was comparable starting at £260 rising to £325 at 18 years. Any cadets with additional academic qualification or able to speak a foreign language received an additional £30 per annum. Throughout the history of Birmingham Police cadets, the girls were always better educationally qualified than male cadets[160].

Angela Harwood has the honour of being the first female cadet in Birmingham City Police. Angela was born in Exmouth Devon in April 1941. There is no explanation why she moved to the Birmingham area but her file informs us that she joined the Birmingham City Police Cadets on the 28th December 1959 as female cadet number one. She is shown as being on the 13th cadet training course, all previous training courses had been for male cadets only. The duties performed by Angela (who had to supply her own black shoes) included accompanying other policewomen to conduct their enquiries and an attachment to the CID in Bradford Street. Angela remained in the cadets and was successful in applying to be an officer in the regular police. On the 8th May 1961 Angela became PW 74 and commenced training at No 4 District Police training centre at Ryton-on-Dunsmore. PW Harwood's career was to be short in Birmingham City Police as there is a letter dated 15/10/64 informing the force that she will be resigning from the service in January 1965 as she wished to emigrate to New Zealand. Her records show that she had a sister living in New Zealand and that she was considering joining New Zealand police. The service record for PW Harwood shows that she resigned at her own request on the 31st January 1965 with her service record shown as exemplary. Angela joined the New Zealand Police in 1965 and was one of the first policewomen in the country to go on the beat, also being recorded as the first female officer in Porirua and later Touranga. Angela reached the rank of inspector and was appointed Community Relations Coordinator for the Manukau district. She did a significant amount of work with young and handicapped people in and outside of work, being awarded the Queen's Service Medal in 1981[161]. After 27 years with the New Zealand Police Angela retired, having done a considerable amount to progress the role of policewomen in the country.

As you would imagine a lot of the training was around discipline with drill and enrolment into Matthew Boulton College for further education. There were differences in the rules and regulations between the sexes. For example the cadets spent time at camp - it was Elan Valley for the boys but the girls initially went to the Ashburton Outward Bound Schools in Devon and then Bishop Abbey in Buckinghamshire. Other locations followed before female cadets also used Elan Valley, although at different times of the year. The girl cadets were treated differently from the boys in other ways too. They could not at first join the regular force until they were 20 years of age whereas the boys could join at 18 years and 9 months until 1961 when it was raised to 19 years. In 1966 the matter was settled when police regulations were changed and both male and female could join as regular members of the force at the age of 19 years.

In 1961, police cadets formed 30% of the intake of recruits to the Birmingham force and the falling off in enlistment was seen as a danger to the force. In that year the establishment of girls was increased to 15. They were seen as a good investment, obviously because of their better qualifications but also because the number not going on to be regular officers was lower than expected.

Four years after the girls had been allowed to join in 1959, 59 girls had enrolled as cadets and 25 were still serving as police women. In 1965 the establishment strength of the cadets was at 150 but by the end of the year there were only 127 members. Recruitment slippage had started, by 1968 the Cadet Corps was only made up of 100 cadets of which 21 were female.

Clearly the ratio for female officers was still improving but there was still a long way to go at a time when recruitment and retention was so difficult. These were the days where there were plenty of jobs around and often better paid. In 1970 for the first time Birmingham City Police were unable to fill all their male vacancies but competition for the female vacancies remained high. The male chauvinists of the time claimed females were attracted by the new uniforms introduced on the 6th June 1970. These are described as being a semi fitted tunic without breast pockets and belts. With an A-line skirt with pleats at the rear and a new style hat to replace the traditional cap. On the 12th July 1970 the Watch Committee agreed to purchase 20 dozen pairs of nylon tights as a sample for the policewomen, together with the normal order of black 30 denier nylon stocking.[162]

Cadets at Tally Ho Police Training Centre c1980

For the earliest 10 female cadet records held by the museum (including some of the very first female cadets in 1959), the average length of service was five years and nine months (not including up to four years spent as a cadet). Five of them left following the birth of their child or other childcare reasons, one to pursue a relationship, one emigrated, one to get a better work/life balance, one transferred and finally one left through ill-health. Eight of them married police officers and a ninth left to continue a relationship with another officer.

An insight into what the cadets did in the 1970s is provided below by Su Handford, one of the museum volunteers who joined the cadets in 1976:

Susan Handford QPM

"On Sunday 15th August 1976, my parents drove me and my suitcase to Tally Ho! Police Training Centre in Birmingham as I had successfully joined the police cadets, fulfilling my dream since I was about three years of age that 'all I want to be when I grow up is a policewoman'. I was shown to my room on the seventh floor, my lovely parents left and apparently my mom cried all the way home.

My school friends were just starting the six weeks holiday from school which I was no longer a part of as I was now employed by the West Midlands Police.

The initial and best part was the fact we were taught self-discipline: the pressing of the shirts 'boxed style', our skirts which were also 'boxed ironed' and the bulling of our shoes which didn't last long after a session on the drill square which is now begrudgingly being used as a car park. Sport played a great part in the cadets as did attending Matthew Boulton Technical College to attain certificates in typing and admin studies, local and central government and many other subjects.

We would also attend Bournville Baths, for swimming lessons and lifesaving coaching and then we would have to run from there back to Tally Ho before lunch, the longer you took to run back the less of your lunch hour you had.

There was also vocational training for cadets by working in the community. I did mine at The Royal Orthopaedic Hospital in Northfield, for a three month period. A month was spent on the Children's Ward, a month in the Men's Ward and a month in theatre. I enjoyed it all so much I was given all the application forms by the nurses and doctors to enrol as a nurse - needless to say that was the last thing I would be doing due to my lifelong ambition to become a police officer. As a 16 year old and being asked and allowed to assist the nurses with the patients and the daily duties, I certainly learnt a lot about life as well as nursing!

There were two cadet camps one for boys and one for girls, this was a gruelling four weeks of canoeing in the freezing water that came from the very bottom of the Elan Valley Dam, mountaineering, abseiling, an assault course, a thorough kit inspection each morning, hard duck boards to sleep on in a huge tent, and many more life challenging issues all whilst away from home for a month. As there were no mobile telephones in those days, every day there would be a rota and a very long queue at the one and only telephone box on the road into camp.

There were also many police attachments you would have to conduct, as I was in the Police Cadets for two and half years I managed to work at those preferred locations for a second time as they were running out of attachments to send me on. The one that stood me in good stead for my career was the attachment to the Coroner's Department, again as a 16-17 year old seeing and experiencing many different aspects of life and death.

In my second year, I was proud to become a squad leader for the next intake of cadets who attended the University of Birmingham for their training. This was a great privilege and honour.

When you were nearing the end of your time as a cadet, you had to perform what was known as a three month beat patrol which I did at Kings Heath Police Station. On my return from Ryton Police Training Centre after ten weeks of training, I was fortunate enough to be posted to B Unit Kings Heath Police Station again, for many, many happy years.

From a police cadet in 1976, little did I think it would give me such a grounding to later be awarded a Queen's Police Medal in my latter service as a police constable. I owe my career to the Police Cadet training."

Su Handford receiving her QPM from the Queen

Love & Marriage

It is not common to find a marriage between two police officers, who both remain in the force until retirement, which goes the distance. The challenging role, unsociable hours, demands of children and close working relationships with colleagues can all contribute to marriage breakdowns, particularly when both individuals within the marriage are police officers.

One of those elusive successful marriages is worth mentioning here. Retired police officers Su and Paul Handford met whilst both were working as cadets and each of them went on to complete 30 years' service. Su went on to receive the QPM (see her story above) and Paul became a Member of the Most Excellent Order of the British Empire (MBE) during his service, reaching the rank of inspector. Su retired in 2011 and Paul retired in 2006. Paul is the current chair of the Military History Society of the West Midlands Police and with their shared passion of the military history of police officers, they both volunteer at the West Midlands Police Museum.

Paul and Su Handford

As stated earlier - only seven records are held by the museum of married women who attained the rank of sergeant or above. Only one of these officers (Evelyn Miles) was already married when they joined. Four of these officers are known to have married other officers. One achieved the rank of inspector and one (Evelyn Unett) chief superintendent.

109 of the 610 female officer records[163] show that the officer resigned to get married. 164 of the women married other officers with the majority of these officers leaving after falling pregnant.

Another couple who recently made headlines in the West Midlands after reaching the significant milestone of 50 years of marriage are Doreen and William (known as Conrad) Joseph.

Conrad and Doreen met when serving in Walsall Borough Police in 1961. Conrad joined Walsall Borough Police as a cadet in 1954. He was based at Walsall and Bloxwich Police Stations, joining the regulars in 1954.

In 1961 he joined the CID and served 25 years up until his retirement in 1986. He was one of the arresting officers in the infamous Raymond Morris case – better known as the Cannock Chase murderer.

His soon to be wife, Doreen Rowley, joined the force in 1961 and served as a PC until 1965 when the pair married.

Their daughter-in-law Joanne Joseph stated "Conrad was standing with his sergeant when he saw Doreen walk by. As soon as he saw her, he said to his boss; 'See that girl there. Well that's the girl I'm going to marry.' And four years later they did!"[164]

Conrad and Doreen with Sergeant Lee Nicholls in 2015

When Walsall officers (including Sergeant Lee Nicolls) found out about the milestone occasion in September 2015, they decided to pay the couple a surprise visit and take them some flowers. They felt they could not let such a special event concerning former fellow officers go unmarked.

Sexuality

There is very little mention of same sex relationships within any of the files in the museum. Bearing in mind that homosexuality was only decriminalised with the Sexual Offences Act 1967 (and even then same sex relationships were only permitted between men over the age of 21 in the privacy of their own homes) it isn't surprising that it doesn't feature much.

Lesbianism has never actually been part of legislation making same sex relationships illegal. There are stories that Queen Victoria wouldn't sign the legislation, as she refused to believe that same sex relationships between women took place. Apparently a Bill to outlaw lesbianism also failed in 1921 because MPs preferred 'to sweep it under the carpet'.[165]

The standards of behaviour for police officers has always been high and anything not widely accepted by society at the time has been unacceptable for officers. Examples in the female officers' files include having a male attend their house who they were not married to, having relationships with married men, or finding themselves in the position of being pregnant outside of marriage. All the officers in these situations were required to resign or strongly encouraged to do so, certainly throughout the first 50 years of female officers. Sometimes the senior officers suspected a female officer was gay, but without evidence simply tried to discourage it and stop other officers gossiping.

Some examples of how female officers were treated when suspected of being gay are given in the files at the museum.

In the file of one female officer who joined the police in 1965 - one of her referees stated she had been a friend of his daughter for many years and had always expressed an interest in being a policewoman. She joined Walsall Borough Police as a cadet in December 1965 and went on to join the regulars of the newly formed West Midlands Constabulary on the 19th December 1966. On the front of her file is clearly marked 'K.I.V. (keep in view) for Regular Force December 1966' which is when she turned 19 and became eligible to become a regular officer. So it would appear the force thought she had potential from an early stage. Her cadet reports show her conduct was always considered exemplary. One of her first training assessments at the

Police Training Centre in Ryton shows she came third in her class and whilst her instructor thought she lacked enthusiasm, said she had the makings of a good police officer. In December 1967 she first submitted an application to resign, with no reason given. Her chief superintendent stated she had become friendly with a WPC from West Bromwich and he believed they wish to start a new life together, hence the resignation. She subsequently withdrew her resignation, stating she had changed her mind. This was accepted and her reports indicate she was trying really hard and her outlook had improved.

In January 1968 it was reported that the WPC from West Bromwich had been staying in this officer's room in the policewomen's hostel and they had been found on two occasions embracing each other and kissing. The WPC had also been told off by the superintendent in charge of the female officers for regularly calling their office and engaging this officer and others in long conversations.

In June 1968 she again applied to resign and this time followed through with it. In July 1969 she applied for a role with the Territorial and Army Reserve and West Midlands Constabulary was asked for a reference as the post involved access to classified information. They subsequently confirmed her service dates but went on to state that the latter part of her service was not satisfactory and they did not recommend her for the role. In November 1970 she applied to work as a traffic warden for Warwickshire and Coventry Constabulary and the reference given by West Midlands Constabulary was similar, but went on to state:

'Whilst in my Force, this officer developed an emotional attachment to another Policewoman, and as a result of this her conduct during the latter part of her service was not entirely satisfactory. Though not discounting the possibility that she has changed, I must say that from knowledge of her I would hesitate to employ her as a Traffic Warden under this Police Authority.'

In February 1970 an article appeared in the Express and Star titled Women in Love Without Men by Laura Gillan[166]. The article is about lesbians and in it are interviews with three women whose names have been changed by the writer. In it 'Susan' talks about having lost her job in a police force when her superintendent found out she was a lesbian. She stated she had applied to share a flat with a friend when she was being posted to another town and her superintendent kept questioning her, so eventually she told her everything and was promptly made to resign. 'Susan' stated she was very bitter about the whole thing, she understood the reputation of the force was important but why did everyone think that that all homosexuals were sexual perverts? 'I find it difficult to accept that now they know what I am, they think I'm going to behave any differently from the way I have for the past two years in the force'. She went on to talk about how difficult it was, having to hide her relationship with her partner from everyone. As far as anyone else was concerned they were friends sharing a flat who sometimes went out for dinner together, but really they wanted to hold hands and not feel on edge all the time, hoping not to be discovered. She finished by stating she wished that their relationship could be accepted and that they could get married in a church. The article concludes by stating the women just want to be accepted for who they are and 'In 1970 is that really too much to ask?' The article appears in this officer's personal file so the conclusion must have been reached previously that she is potentially 'Susan'.

Interestingly the article also appears in the file of the WPC from West Bromwich who was told off for constantly calling the first officer. The West Bromwich officer was going through disciplinary proceedings in relation to her close relationship with the other officer ('which was the subject of much gossip') and her failure to follow orders and apparent need for close supervision. She left the force slightly earlier than the other officer in May 1968 and it would appear stayed in contact with her – she also applied to the Territorial and Army Reserve in 1969 but received the same reference from West Midlands Constabulary.

1970s – Amalgamation and Integration

Only a handful of files for officers who joined in the 1970s are held by the museum – all of those having relatively short careers. Most of the files for officers who joined at this time or later are still considered 'live' files and are therefore not available to the museum, even where the officers may have long since retired.

Amalgamation

On the 1st April 1974 Birmingham City Police was merged with West Midlands Constabulary, parts of Warwickshire & Coventry Constabulary, parts of Staffordshire County & Stoke-on-Trent Constabulary and parts of West Mercia Constabulary to become West Midlands Police.

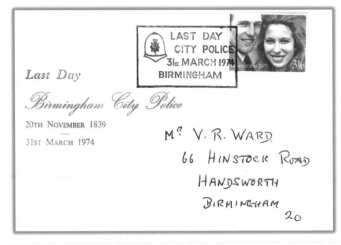

One of only 3000 envelopes with a commemorative stamp from the last day of the Birmingham City Police

The first Chief Constable appointed to head West Midlands Police was Sir Derrick Capper, the last Chief Constable of Birmingham City Police.

When the new force came into being on 1st April it was 17.5% under strength. Various measures were taken to improve the situation including £24,000 to promote recruitment in the form of press and television advertisements, liaison with schools and employment agencies and stands at exhibitions. The force also benefited from the national recruiting campaign on which over £682,000 was spent in 1974/5.[167]

Pauline Campbell-Moss

The summer of 1974 saw the arrival of the West Midlands' first black or minority ethnic (BME) female officer. Pauline Campbell (as she was known then) made history when she joined West Midlands Police as a cadet.

An article in The Voice from 8/11/2015[168] states Pauline moved with her family to Handsworth from Jamaica when she was nine and she had always dreamed of being a police officer. With her initials being PC she felt it was her destiny!

She also clearly remembers the day she sat her exam in Birmingham. She stated "We took the test and we were told to wait until the names of those who had passed were called out".

"Mine was the third name to be announced, but when the officer saw me he took one look at me and said: 'No, not you. Sit down!'

"I kept standing up and when he asked me why, I said to him: 'I'm standing because you called my name.'"

After discussions with colleagues the officer reluctantly nodded Pauline through and her career began as a rookie police recruit. "I felt the officer had exposed his own personal prejudice towards me, but I expected that. It didn't faze me."

She experienced a lot of difficulty because of her ethnicity, from members of the public who often referred to her as 'the coloured girl'. She recalls two incidents in particular – one where she was threatened by youths with knives on a bus and one where she was actually bundled into the back of a car and had to escape by throwing herself out whilst the car was still moving.

She left after three years to work with social services in Birmingham where she felt better able to support troubled youths.

By 2017 she lived in New York and worked in a prison ministry.

Sex Discrimination Act 1975

When the Sex Discrimination Act was passed in 1975, many police forces were still paying female police officers a percentage of a male officer's wage, including West Midlands Police. The legislation made it illegal to pay women less for doing the same job and the force took immediate action, bringing female officers' pay in line with male officers for the first time.

Christine Read

Christine became the first female officer to undertake motorcycle patrol in October 1978.

Elizabeth Dodd

Liz joined Birmingham City Police in May 1972. She had a great mix of jobs on the E and F divisions starting in the Police Women's Department at Bromford Lane, then Hay Mills before the new Stechford station opened. She recalls as a policewoman receiving less pay than male colleagues, only dealing with women and children, only being allocated an unmarked car and occasionally working nights.

When West Midlands Police implemented equal pay, everything changed and she was really pleased.

Liz felt she could go out and be a proper police officer; undertake a mix of jobs, shifts and take the opportunity for different roles. After several applications to be a dog handler - some returned or just torn up saying "what do you want to do this for", in June 1979, Liz Dodd joined the E Division dog section and became the first female dog handler to work in the West Midlands Police. But she had to train locally as there weren't facilities for women to train at Stafford!

Police Dog Czar was allocated to Liz for almost 6 years and she had a great time moving to Bridge Street West, which mainly covered Digbeth. Liz states 'in real terms as the 'dog man' you were sent anywhere, off division even off the force area sometimes. There was an element of freedom but lots of trust too because you answered to the force control room and the local controller.'

After PD Czar retired, Liz remained at Digbeth as a uniformed officer before

working on collating stolen vehicles.

Liz says her intention had been to work her 30 years for her pension and on retirement lock the front door of her Solihull apartment and drive off to Europe in her motor home. However on 1st March 1986 with a CID colleague she went to collect a female from Erdington station to bring back to Digbeth and on their return they were involved in a road traffic collision. She received multiple injuries and never returned to work. She left West Midlands Police in August 1987 on an ill health pension.

1980s – Branching Out

Angie Clamp

Angie (far left) began her policing career in May 1979 when, aged 21, she joined West Midlands Police after leaving The Royal Navy.

She did her probationary period at West Bromwich and also worked from Old Hill Police Station. After her probation was complete she applied and was successful in moving to

Coventry (her home town). She was on shift as a foot officer and also a panda driver before moving to the local beat office and then early in 1984 applied for the Underwater Search Unit.

She became the first female officer to be posted to the unit in the West Midlands. When she joined the unit was operating on a part time basis but not long after she qualified it went full time and Angie was fortunate enough to become a member of the full time unit.

This unit ran until 1999 when it was disbanded. In 2004 a shallow water search capability was established within the Operational Support Unit in the Operations Department. It was established in response to a fire service decision to stop recovering bodies from water - this team are capable of recovering bodies floating in any depth of water and can also conduct searches of water on foot up to chest depth. If the force requires an underwater search capability Nottinghamshire Police's Dive Team are used – this is a very rare occasion maybe once or twice a year.

Angie competed in swimming, lifesaving and water polo for the police whilst she served. She was later injured traveling to work and as a result had to leave the Underwater Search Unit and returned to the beat office in Coventry before being forced to retire on an ill health pension in April 1997. In those days there was no role for a restricted officer.

Angie said of her time in policing: 'In my day they if there was a bar fight, they would send policewomen in first to calm the situation, no one would hit a WPC. The same cannot be said anymore. The highlight of my career was definitely being part of the Underwater Search Unit.'

Kay Weale

WPC Kay Weale joined the West Midlands Police in March 1980. When she went for her initial interview to join the force in 1979 she was asked if she had any leanings towards any particular department. When she mentioned either Mounted Branch or Dog Unit she was told "Put it out of your mind my dear, we don't have women in either of those departments." Oh how things changed!

In October 1984 Kay began her training with the Mounted Branch of West Midlands Police and when she transferred in June 1985 she officially became the first mounted female officer in the West Midlands Police.

By the time she left in 1997 the Mounted Branch contained several female officers. Kay recalls one of her proudest moments was following a particularly violent football match when bricks had been flying and chaos ruled. They finally got back to base and

one of the previously extremely "anti-female on the branch" officers put his arms around her and Jo Dix (the second girl on the branch) and said "I absolutely hate to have to admit this but I was as happy to have you two at my side today as any other member of the branch!" Kay states that was praise indeed!

Kay absolutely loved her time on the Mounted Branch and broke down in tears when told she had to leave following an injury on duty. She describes it as being like she lost a part of herself, the job on the branch was such a huge part of her life. She says she would give anything to be able to go back and do it all again. She recalls being very sad when the division was eventually disbanded in 1999 and was glad that she wasn't actually there to see it happen.

Shindo Barquer

West Midlands Police recruited its first female Sikh officer when Shindo Barquer joined and she worked her way up the ranks to Chief Inspector. In doing so she became the first female BME officer to attain this rank. Shindo has worked in various operational and specialist roles and has been involved in the development of others, she is also a qualified mentor.

1990s – A Turbulent Time for Policing

The 1990s was a very turbulent time for West Midlands Police and for policing in general, including several key events:

- 1991 the Birmingham Six were released from prison, following the quashing of their convictions in 1975 for the Birmingham Pub Bombings that occurred in 1974

- Investigation of South Yorkshire Police's handling of the Hillsborough disaster through the early 1990s
- Creation of many different electronic information systems for different areas of policing
- 1995 also saw the introduction of the world's first national DNA database when the UK database was created. This followed the UK's first conviction using DNA, when Colin Pitchfork was convicted of rape and murder in 1988.

Liz Crawley

In March 1990 Liz Crawley transferred to the force's Driving Unit to become West Midlands Police's first female driving instructor. She joined the force in April 1977 where she remained a police constable until October 1993.

She states it was the highlight of her career when she qualified and transferred on to the driving school, made even more special as she was following in her father's footsteps, as he had also been a police driving instructor. Although they never served together as he retired in 1976.

She states she was fully aware of animosity from older male colleagues shown towards her and other female officers. In her early days, it was quite common for female officers to have their bottoms smacked and be the butt of sexual innuendoes. When challenged, action was rarely

taken against the perpetrator. It was still very much a male dominated profession and she felt that for any woman to progress in a specialised department she would have to work twice as hard as her male counterpart, to be considered his equal. By the time she left, she states attitudes had changed enormously: 'the old stalwarts had long since retired and young male officers accepted the fact that equality was the order of the day'.

Kerry Delaney

In 1990 the Operational Support Unit (OSU) got its first female officer – not just in the West Midlands but across the whole of the UK (the Metropolitan Police had female OSU officers at this time but they played a more paramedic type role). Kerry Delaney joined West Midlands Police in 1983 and remained until 1994 when she transferred to Lancashire.

Kerry recalls seeing the post advertised for a male or female officer and thought it was just an equal opportunities tick box exercise, but decided to apply anyway. Initially she failed the fitness test as she was recovering from an 18 month illness but she passed the interview and was found suitable for the job. Three months later she passed the fitness test with flying colours and began her new job on the 25th June 1990.

She states she approached the OSU crew room on her first day nervously – she was after all the only female in a department of 140 men! She found that her apprehension was groundless – she was accepted immediately and expected to be as involved in all operations as her male colleagues.

She was finally able to attend Public Order training, which she had been excluded from for years because she was a woman, and she was immediately put onto an intermediate driving course to allow her to drive the OSU van (or the big wagon – as it was known to local drug dealers!).

Her work involved keeping observations on drug dens with her crew – arresting individuals involved in drug deals, tackling prostitution and the rising problem of 'jammers' – who would steal from victims waiting in their cars at red traffic lights.

Kerry remembers the most important thing in the OSU as being the team ethos – she worked well with all of her partners whilst on the OSU and everyone stuck together to support each other, get the job done and deliver a professional service.

In an interview with force magazine The Manager she stated she would use her feminine charm to dispel customers having difficulty leaving licensed premises at closing time, which was one of the areas of work the unit were involved in.

She was soon joined by other female colleagues in 1991 – she is pictured below along with PC Karen Audley and Sergeant Linda Boyle who was the first female sergeant on the OSU:

Left to right: PC Kerry Delaney, PC Karen Audley and Sergeant Lynda Boyle

Upon leaving the OSU after completing three years there, Kerry states 'there is definitely a place for females on the OSU and it isn't just for making the tea, although as every new boy, sorry person, will tell you – that will be one of your first tasks!'

Julia Walsh

Julia's start date with West Midlands Police was the 8th August 1980. She was a cadet the year before, joining in August 1979. She retired in May 2011 at the rank of detective inspector having completed 31 years' service.

Julia states "I thoroughly enjoyed my police career and it shaped the person I am today. The police force was obviously male dominated when I joined. I remember I was really keen to transfer to CID but soon realised that although I had completed a successful CID attachment I would only be transferred if the existing sole female detective left the department! Fortunately for me she left just as I was finishing my attachment so I transferred immediately making me then the only female detective in the department dealing with the obvious female related offences of rape and other sexual assaults together with the general crime the males were dealing with."

Julia recalls her colour was something she did not dwell on or exploit. She joined to be a police officer not a black police officer. She was very against positive discrimination, always believing that ability was the thing that mattered over everything else.

When she was promoted to sergeant in 1991 she really tried to avoid a fuss but felt under pressure and duty bound to allow the force to highlight her promotion in the press. Looking back now, Julia states she feels very proud to have made history as the first black female sergeant.

Pat Barnett

Pat Barnett was the very first female officer to hold the rank of Assistant Chief Constable (ACC) in the West Midlands after it was announced she would act as ACC (Inspectorate) for a six month spell from August 1991, to cover another ACC's secondment to another project[169].

She joined Birmingham City Police on the 11th October 1966 where she remained until the 1st February 1970. She then transferred to Warwickshire & Coventry Constabulary for four years until Coventry was amalgamated into West Midlands Police, when she held the rank of inspector.

In 1988 as a superintendent she was seconded to West Mercia for 12 months where the following glowing account of her initial progress was given:

'The anticipated novelty by the Division of the appointment of a female Deputy Divisional Commander who, in addition, is perhaps the most academically qualified in the country and the only one in the rank to have a young child was quickly forgotten. Her pleasant, humorous personality and astute professionalism soon displaced such side issues.'

She returned to West Midlands Police and in 1991 became acting Assistant Chief Constable.

Acting Assistant Chief Constable Pat Barnett: now breaking new ground.

In January 1996 after 29 years and 110 days' service Pat retired from the police service on superannuation.

Vanessa Carroll

In 1996 tragedy struck when West Midlands Police experienced its first fallen female officer. The only earlier female officer on the force's Roll of Honour was Mary Baldwin of Birmingham City Police.

Inspector Vanessa Carroll, aged 35, was killed in a road accident whilst serving with the Western European Union Police based in Mostar, Bosnia, on the 28th April 1996.

Vanessa was serving as part of a multinational group who were tasked with reviewing proposed policing arrangements in support of Civil Administration in Mostar, Bosnia–Herzegovina, and unifying the local police, which had been split during the civil war.

Vanessa had completed 16 years exemplary service. She started her police career with the West Midlands Police as a cadet at the age of just 16 in 1977. She joined the regulars on 8th September 1979. She was posted to the L division at Chelmsley Wood Police Station.

One of Vanessa's closest friends Deb Menzel recalls 'Vanessa was a really kind person, she would go out of her way to help anyone who needed help, she had a strong sense of right and wrong that helped make her an outstanding officer. A real bobby's bobby - she was a workaholic. She always looked immaculate. She also loved sports - Vanessa was captain of the force's netball team and she was a very fit cross country runner. I lost count at the amount of prisoners she chased and caught in the early days of her career when we shared the same shift and walked the beat together. They were very happy days.'

In 1985 Vanessa passed her sergeants exams and she went to be a sergeant at Queens Road Police Station in Aston. She later moved into CID and spent some time as a detective sergeant on various squads. Wherever she went she was successful and incredibly well liked and respected by her colleagues.

In 1994 she was promoted to inspector and returned to Chelmsley Wood where it all started for her.

Deb states 'She was a fantastic shift inspector. She was strict and fair, demanding a high work load from every member of her team, they worked hard and played hard and always got good results.'

She was a good friend to a lot of people, including her work friends and her team mates in sport. She is certainly fondly remembered by any officer who worked alongside her.

Deb states 'I consider it a privilege to have known her. Vanessa was a very talented lady. There was nothing she could not achieve, she was an outstanding officer and a friend in a million who was an inspiration to myself and so many others'.

Anne Summers QPM

In 1996 Anne Summers made history by becoming the West Midlands' first substantive female Assistant Chief Constable when she was promoted from Avon and Somerset Constabulary to West Midlands Police, beating four other (male) candidates to the job.

She started her policing career in Bristol in what was then the Bristol Constabulary (also known as the Bristol City Police) in 1971. She recalls that at this time women had just received a pay increase to bring them up to 95% of male officers' salary, from the previous position of 90%.

At the time Anne joined, most forces were not able to recruit more than 5% of their establishment as women – with the exception of certain city forces such as Birmingham, Liverpool, Manchester and the Metropolitan Police who had their own percentages calculated based on the size of their force.

She remembers being surprised and disappointed after coming out of the police training school to realise that she would be in a separate Women's Police Department. The female officers dealt solely with what would now be referred to as public protection work - domestic violence and child abuse.

Anne has many memories of the 1970s driving round in Morris 1000 panda cars as the female officers had to attend any arrest of a woman. Because the cars only had two doors, she would always end up being shoved in the back seat with the prisoner, which could be quite challenging when the prisoner was clamouring to get out of the vehicle!

In the 1974 amalgamations she became part of Avon & Somerset Constabulary. She then went onto the Bristol Crime Squad and became a sergeant quite early in her career in 1976, a week after the Sex Discrimination Act came in, where only weeks before the force had increased women's salaries up to 100% of their male counterparts. She states the police, like the Army, had suspected they would not be subject to sex discrimination legislation and were surprised to find that they were. However in Avon and Somerset they did manage to bring women's pay in line with men prior to being legally obliged to under the legislation. At 24, she was the youngest sergeant in the force and one of the youngest in the country.

When she was promoted to inspector in 1984 she became the first operational female inspector in Avon and Somerset. She recalls that women didn't get truncheons until the early 1980s in Avon and Somerset, but like many other forces they were issued with a handbag, which she found a ridiculous concept for a female officer on patrol and most of them were later returned completely unused.

Anne came to West Midlands Police in 1996 as an Assistant Chief Constable (ACC) with responsibility for the Community Affairs & Planning portfolio. She was the only female candidate and never thought she would be successful.

She recalls on the morning of her interview she read a newspaper with a headline stating that West Midlands Police was the worst performing force in the country at the time, which stuck in her mind for the interview!

She later became the ACC in charge of the 'crime' portfolio, with responsibility for criminal investigation and intelligence. This role she really enjoyed. Here she experienced one of the highlights of her policing career with the successful prosecution and subsequent imprisonment of two known paedophiles, following a long and expensive undercover operation which managed to prevent a child abduction, sexual assault and murder. This all stemmed from the recommendations of a female inspector working in child abuse investigation about some individuals being released from prison. She was incredibly proud of her team – as it was Easter she bought them eggs to celebrate and they later invited her to the celebratory drinks.

There was one amusing moment in Anne's career after arriving in the West Midlands, when her uniform was covered with a coat and her rank could not be identified. She was in the lift at the police headquarters at Lloyd House going up to the 11th floor (the Command Team floor) and a male officer got in and said 'What floor darling?' to which she replied '11th please and I'm not your darling'! He later came to her office to apologise which she found amusing, albeit unnecessary.

Anne recalls another highlight of her career was seeing the changes delivered under the late 1990s restructure of the force. Things had to change and although it was very hard for some people, things worked out for the better and it was very rewarding seeing the changes in action – including CID officers being back out on divisions and multi-function crime scene investigators, as opposed to individual roles for each element of crime scene investigation.

One of the most disturbing times she can remember is when people told her they didn't tell anyone they worked for West Midlands Police because they were embarrassed. This was at the very start of her WMP career and should be taken into context with recent policing events from the time including the downfall of the Serious Crime Squad and the release of the 'Birmingham Six'.

Chief Constable Edward Crew arrived a couple of months after Anne started in the West Mids. When Lloyd House was refurbished a few years later and his office was extended, she states it was so long it reminded her of a bowling alley! So she took a skittles set and when he arrived for his first day in his new office he was surprised to find the whole Command Team playing ten pin bowling!

In 1999 she became the Deputy Chief Constable – another female first for the West Midlands.

When she retired in 2002 she states the farewells and the warmth and kindness from officers and staff across different departments was truly overwhelming. She recalls the drivers from Park Lane presenting her with a crystal figure of a horse and she was also presented with a shield including the badges of all three of the forces she had worked for.

Sarah Walker

In 1998 PC Sarah Walker made history by becoming the first female constable attached to the Air Support Unit in West Midlands Police.

She joined West Midlands Police on the 16th of September 1992 and was one of only a handful of female air operations officers across the whole country. Sarah was 23 years old at the time, and it was something that she had set her heart on.

Now Sarah Hipkins, she is still serving in the police as an investigation officer at Wolverhampton Central Police Station. During her years with the force she has undertaken a number of different roles. She started on a shift at Birmingham Road Police Station in Wolverhampton, but always aspired to be an air observer. She never actually expected to achieve that dream.

When Sarah joined the police it was a very male dominated environment and up until that point there had not been any female officers who worked within the Aviation Team - which had been operating for a number of years. It was with some trepidation that she applied for the post, feeling that she had nothing to lose. She was young in service and had no background of serving in the military or working with helicopters. There were a number of assessments to be completed before she was successful in getting the job and she recalls that they were not the easiest of things to pass.

Over the years, in general, Sarah has seen policing change for the better for female officers. There is more respect inside the force for them than there used to be. She has also seen and benefited from the introduction of flexible working arrangements for part-time officers. As a mum of three young children, married to a serving Army officer, this goes some way to allow her to juggle a number of balls in the air at one time. Without it, she says she probably wouldn't still be able to work for the police.

Ashley Moore

Whilst Ashley wasn't the first female armed officer in West Midlands Police, she was the first female to be posted to an armed response vehicle (ARV) after joining the Firearms Operations Unit (FOU). The few that preceded her were based at Birmingham Airport.

Initially Ashley joined the force as a cadet in 1990 where she remained for two years. She states she never wanted to be a police officer as a child, even though her father and uncle worked for the West Midlands Police and her mother had previously worked for Birmingham City Police, leaving to have Ashley's older brother. She saw an advert for police cadets and saw it as an opportunity to earn £400 a month so applied!

Ashley joined the regular officers on the 16th September 1992 at 18 years of age. She did her first few roles in Birmingham, working in a response role, on the Vehicle Squad and also assisting with the investigation of the murder of Nicola Dixon in Sutton Coldfield.

In 1996 she started the process of applying to become an Authorised Firearms Officer (AFO), a long and challenging process that wasn't complete until 1998 when she was posted to Birmingham Airport. Ashley was very young in service for a firearms officer but that didn't put her off. Nor did the fact that the only other female officer on the various courses she had to complete was unsuccessful at an early stage. She felt that she had a point to prove and needed to go above and beyond what was required – being a female coming into a male dominated area where not many females had worked previously, she states she didn't want anyone to believe she had only been successful because she was female.

In April 2000 Ashley was posted to the ARV team. She states that the FOU initially struggled to know how to deal with having a female officer. For example to get to the crew room you had to walk through the locker room which of course was full of male officers' lockers. She states the unit literally cleared out a cleaning cupboard and put her locker in there.

She feels that the whole unit, the way they operate, train and recruit has come on in leaps and bounds since she started there.

Ashley states that for her, the one thing that has changed the most is how the department tries to recruit and retain female officers within the FOU. One of the first jobs she did when she started was to send out a letter to every female officer in the force, asking if they were interested in joining! Now the unit has changed how it markets itself, has shown that it is not only a place for male officers to work and tries very hard to retain female officers through implementing flexible working or part time working arrangements. In particular Ashley feels the FOU were really supportive through both of her pregnancies, letting her remain on the unit in a restricted capacity rather than posting her somewhere else and allowing her to come back on a part time basis until her second child was at pre-school.

Ashley has had many career highs, several from being a 'close protection trained' officer which has given her duties such as being the personal protection officer to the Kurdish Prime Minister during the Olympics in 2012, going to Buckingham Palace and being one of several close protection officers for the Queen when she visited in 2015. Her highlight is when she first made it on to the unit as the competition was so fierce and the physical fitness requirements were incredibly high. It was a real achievement for her.

Ashley did her firearms instructor course in February 2015 and still works within the FOU as an instructor. She is married to another ARV officer who joined the unit after their marriage and they have two children.

From 2000 Onwards

West Midlands Association for Women in Policing

In 2004, a group of women identified the need for a more formalised network for women within West Midlands Police. A number of issues were identified, affecting not only women but other employees, which required a more corporate response.

West Midlands Association for Women in Policing (WMAWP) has been developed in line with the aims and objectives of the British Association for Women in Policing (BAWP). BAWP is the national association for women, formed in 1987, and was the foundation for the establishment of WMAWP at regional level. WMAWP was constitutionalised in 2007.

The overall strategic aim of the association is **"to encourage and enable the women of West Midlands Police to make their full contribution to policing"**. WMAWP gives members an opportunity to make their voice heard, they are regularly asked for their input and feedback on various issues which affect women within the force.

Membership of WMAWP is open to everyone, both female and male, police officers, special constables, PCSOs and staff.

Deborah Adele Harman-Burton

In 2006 the force lost another female officer who has been remembered on the Roll of Honour. Deborah Harman-Burton was killed in a road accident whilst travelling home from night duty - aged 28, on the 24th March.

Born in November 1977, Debbie Harman joined West Midlands Police on 26th August 2003. She worked as an officer in Coventry and was described as hardworking, conscientious and popular by her peers.

PC Harman was a passenger in a Renault Clio involved in a collision on the A452 near Kenilworth. Her partner, who was the driver, was seriously injured in the three-car incident.

Her chief superintendent stated 'her commitment to serving the residents of Coventry had been formally recognised on more than one occasion with Chief Superintendent's Commendations for bravery and reducing crime against Coventry's students'.[170]

Lesbian, gay, bisexual and transgender officers (LGBT)

For many years, the police service and the state were at odds with LGBT people, and there existed pieces of legislation that meant that LGBT people did not enjoy the same rights as non-LGBT people. The LGBT community viewed the police with suspicion, and most interactions were very negative, often resulting in arrests under what is now outdated and repealed legislation. Police forces proactively targeted gay men in known cruising areas, often employing covert tactics to coerce men in to committing public decency or public order offences in order to get an easy arrest and detection.

Hate crime against LGBT people wasn't even recognised in law until 2003, and even to this day it remains hugely under reported.

The Gay Police Association was established in London in 1990 against a background of significant institutional homophobia within the Metropolitan Police and other forces. It would be ten years before West Midlands Police established its own group.

West Midlands Police Rainbow Network was established in 2000, after two of its female officers had their relationship blessed. This was long before civil partnerships and equal marriage came in to play, and it was simply a blessing. Someone at the officers' station leaked the news of the blessing to the press and for a few days there was a media circus with the story being carried as headline news by a number of tabloid news outlets.

There were press camped outside the station, and one of the couple was followed around by reporters whilst carrying out her day to day duties. A member of the police authority at the time was quoted in the papers as saying the public of the West Midlands wanted to be policed by normal people – people like them, and there was no place for gay people in the police.

The chair of the police authority, the now late Bob Jones, sought to distance the authority from these comments, and went on record to congratulate the couple and wrote to them to apologise for the comments of his board member, stating that they didn't reflect the broader view of West Midlands Police. Bob remained throughout the rest of his life, a firm supporter of LGBT equality in policing.

There was a small support network around the two officers, and this support was channelled in to asking the force if an LGBT support network could be established. At this point, the Black and Asian Police Association and Women in Policing already existed, so the concept of staff associations was nothing new. Eventually the force agreed to the creation of a staff association for LGBT staff and Rainbow Network was born.

Over the years, as LGBT equality has gained ground, and the workforce has become more and more diverse and inclusive, the need for support internally dropped off. The association went through a rebrand and changed its name to 'The LGBT Network' and shifted focus on working with the public to increase reporting of hate crime and same-sex domestic abuse and honour based violence.

Chair of the WMP LGBT Network PC Gary Stack said 'There's still a part to play in supporting colleagues, and we recently introduced an Allies scheme that saw our membership numbers swell to well over 1000 people.

West Midlands Police LGBT Network is now the largest LGBT police staff association in the UK, and its activities include raising awareness, training new police officers and staff with a particular focus on transgender issues, and working with communities to improve relations between them and the police.'

Suzette Davenport QPM

Suzette started her career with West Mercia Police and worked there for 20 years before undertaking a short attachment at the Home Office in 2005. She transferred to Staffordshire Police as an Assistant Chief

Constable and in May 2007 Suzette joined West Midlands Police and became their second substantive female Assistant Chief Constable. She led on intelligence and local policing, also being the senior officer responsible for the Management of Police Information programme – which addressed concerns raised under the Bichard enquiry into the tragic deaths of Holly Wells and Jessica Chapman in Soham in 2002.

In August 2010 she went to Northamptonshire as their Deputy Chief Constable and eventually became Gloucestershire Constabulary's first female Chief Constable in February 2013[171].

Suzette has a keen interest in diversity issues and was the vice-chair of the British Association of Women in Policing for eight years.

She made headlines in June 2014 when she told the crowd at Gloucestershire's gay pride event that she was gay, making her the first openly gay Chief Constable. She was commended for her bravery in sharing something so personal at such a public event.

In 2016 she received the Queen's Policing Medal for her services to policing.

Suzette Davenport after receiving her QPM, October 2016

Sharon Rowe QPM

Sharon joined the Metropolitan Police Service in May 1984. Policing was very topical at this time. The Police College at Hendon was being utilised as a deployment base for public order officers on the miners' strike and just weeks before Sharon joined the police service, Metropolitan Police officer WPC Yvonne Fletcher was shot dead outside the Libyan Embassy. Sharon, who grew up in Gloucestershire, says she didn't appreciate at the time how concerned her family must have felt, although throughout her career her family were fully supportive of her career choice.

Sharon went on to serve 25 years in the Metropolitan Police. She undertook a variety of uniform and detective roles, working in outer and inner London. She had experienced a good cross-section of areas of operational policing which she believes is extremely important in being able to be a confident and competent leader.

It was 1994, ten years into her service, before Sharon went for her first promotion and was successful in achieving the rank of sergeant. Up to this point she had really enjoyed shift work, was part of a great team and didn't really have anyone encouraging her to think about career ambitions. The main reason she applied for promotion was after seeing other sergeants carrying out their duties and thinking 'I can do better than that'. Until this point Sharon didn't have the confidence to put herself forward, which she feels is partly due to working with some exceptional officers that made her think she hadn't reached the required standard. Sharon would go on to mentor many officers and police staff.

On promotion to inspector she was posted to the Central London Crime Squad that was low on female officers. To start with she thought it would be really challenging to manage a very experienced, male dominated squad however she really valued her time there. The department dealt with serious and organised crime across London which required painstaking detailed investigations. This is when Sharon's passion for criminal intelligence and its usage started to grow. She oversaw the use of intelligence within the command and realised the critical importance intelligence plays when working really closely with investigative teams. In her experience she thinks that often uniform and detective roles can forget the value that each other can bring and there is a need for more cross fertilisation across uniform and specialist departments.

As a detective chief inspector, Sharon was on one of the original national working groups that developed the National Intelligence Model throughout 1998 and 1999. She was then given the not so insignificant job of implementing the model across the Metropolitan Police! She went on to lead the MPS intelligence unit and in 2003 was working with national and international law enforcement partners in designing computer automated criminal nominal and network profiling which assessed their threat, harm and risk.

Sharon became a chief superintendent in 2005 and returned to local policing. She was subsequently posted to Enfield – which also happened to be where she lived – which helped her to develop a true understanding of the impact of crime and disorder on local communities and the importance of community policing and working with local partners.

In 2007 she became the chief superintendent with responsibility for Lambeth. This borough had the highest murder and gun crime rate in London with significant problems in relation to drug use, gang violence and most importantly the trust and confidence issues between the community and the local police. Sharon believes it is really important to understand the history of an area and know about the significant events in that location, before you can be expected to police it with any authority. She believes in getting out and speaking to different people in the community who will give an honest, if sometimes negative, view on policing. It was at this point that Sharon learnt the value of building trust and relationships with community leaders – something which stood her in good stead later in her career in the West Midlands. An example of this is briefing community leaders before a policing operation is carried out in a sensitive area of the borough. There is clearly a risk involved in this but it evidently demonstrates the value of the relationship between the police and the community. At community meetings she remembers a number of difficult sensitive conversations debating why young men were being murdered and how collectively everyone had a responsibility to stop the violence.

Sharon gave out her telephone number to key individuals and would take calls day and night, even on holidays abroad, signifying the importance of building trusting relationships with the community. She says 'Some postings are 24/7, you become emotionally connected.'

Sharon completed the Senior Command Course in February 2009 and in June that year transferred to West Midlands Police. She wanted a new challenge of working in a different force and on reflection she feels this gave her a wider breadth of experience and expertise as a Chief Officer.

During the next five years Sharon held a variety of portfolios and also managed a number of change programmes one of which was the centralisation of all the call handling centres. She led a variety of successful large scale operations such as the visit of Pope Benedict XVI in 2010, policing the Olympics in 2012 and several

English Defence League demonstrations. She also played a significant role on Project Champion in 2010 and during the August riots in 2011. She had continued to build close relationships with community representatives which she again would say was critical during these events.

She has endeavoured to ensure the force understands the value of community feedback and engagement with the community at the earliest opportunity. The most important aspect of policing for Sharon is to ensure the community has a voice, the freedom to talk and the ability to be heard. Even if they are saying something that is difficult for the police to hear.

In 2013 Sharon was promoted to Temporary Deputy Chief Constable. She had continued her national work on intelligence throughout her career. She now held the ACPO portfolio for the National Intelligence Model and was also an advisor to the newly formed National Crime Agency assisting with the design and implementation of a national tasking and co-ordination framework for all UK law enforcement agencies.

Sharon retired in 2014 and was awarded the Queen's Police Medal for distinguished service. Her legacy would be to have transformed the role intelligence plays in policing and enhanced community engagement across the West Midlands. Her leadership was inspirational to many.

Sally Bourner

Sally Bourner, age 4

Sally started on D Unit at Steelhouse Lane Police Station in 1990. Her initial impressions of policing when she started her career were those of camaraderie and team spirit, and the distinct lack of women in specialist roles and leadership positions.

Sally states for her, what has changed the most for women is the expansion of opportunities with women increasingly represented in every role and at every level. She has too many career highlights to mention, but she would focus on:

'The theme of **PEOPLE**: the public – I will always remember the countless people I and colleagues have helped often in the most difficult and life changing of circumstances, and colleagues – every day I am privileged to work alongside colleagues whose care and commitment for the work they do gives me my unbridled energy, passion and pride for policing. If I had to pick ONE highlight it would be my time as the Solihull LPU Commander because it was a time when everything I love came together – changing lives; local policing; working in partnership to prevent crime and harm, and as a leader the challenge and buzz that comes from balancing a wide range of complex and competing demands every day.'

Sally is a very positive LGBT role model within West Midlands Police. She recalls that she 'came out' in 1995 when she was a sergeant. There were two reasons why she felt able to 'come out' at that time and openly be herself ever since:

1) Her incredible and supportive network of family, friends and colleagues.

2) Her wish to be authentic in every aspect of her life – Stonewall say very powerfully that 'people perform better when they can be themselves'. Sally states 'I wanted to be me in every aspect of my life including at work. I am confident that people across West Midlands Police will tell you that I am first and foremost a genuine and caring person who comes into work to make a difference; that I am a trusted and effective police officer who happens to be a woman and openly gay.'

Whilst she does not come into work to be a role model, she takes her responsibilities as a woman and an openly gay woman very seriously because the influence she can bring as a senior officer to help others (often those who she has never met) is significant. She was helped and supported by two colleagues (now friends) in the mid 1990's, Anne Summers (WMP Deputy Chief Constable) and Cressida Dick (Commissioner of the Metropolitan Police Service) who made time to help and support her. The influence they had in the importance of making time for others is a key reason why she now takes time to coach, mentor and support others at all levels across WMP. Sally says as a leader giving back is key.

In 2014 the West Midlands Police Museum Committee appointed its first female chair when Sally agreed to take on the role. Sally's passion and enthusiasm has kept the museum going over the past few years and certainly helped to raise its profile. She does her utmost to preserve the heritage of West Midlands Police and its various predecessor forces. She takes every opportunity to highlight the value the museum adds to modern day policing and how important it is that we do not forget the origins of policing in the Midlands and how far we have come.

Female leaders

In 2014 West Midlands Police was making headlines due to the significant number of female officers and staff heading up departments and local policing units.[172] With a female Temporary Deputy Chief Constable, Deputy Police and Crime Commissioner, Head of Legal Services and eight female chief superintendents leading departments and local policing units as well as numerous other senior officer and staff roles, the force was able to visibly demonstrate its commitment to equality and diversity.

Front row left to right: Lisa-Marie Smith, Head of Legal Services, Chief Superintendent Emma Barnett, T/Deputy Chief Constable Sharon Rowe,

Deputy Police and Crime Commissioner Yvonne Mosquito, Police and Crime Commissioner Bob Jones.

Back row left to right: Chief Superintendent Claire Bell, Chief Superintendent Rachel Jones, Chief Superintendent Sharon Goosen and T/Chief Superintendent Jo Smallwood.

Michele Larmour

ACC Michele Larmour joined West Midlands Police in June 2015, having completed her previous 28 years of police service in Northern Ireland.

Michele joined the Royal Ulster Constabulary GC in 1986 as a young country girl from rural Tyrone, heading off to the police training centre in the city of Belfast. Thirty years later she finds it hard to believe she is now executive lead for Local Policing across the West Midlands, an area with a population of three million including the second largest city in England.

During her initial training, she achieved the school's prize - the academic prize given to the highest scoring student. She recalls training as militaristic with a strict regime of show parades, word perfect definitions and new officers were 'recruits'. She reminisces on the rectangle black handbag she was issued, a piece of police equipment she never used!

She remembers looking up in awe at the office where the chief superintendent who was in charge of all of the training was based. Ironically before she took the job in West Midlands Police, she *was* the chief superintendent in charge of training and development in PSNI, sitting in that very office.

Michele was posted first to Newry in County Down. It had experienced a mortar attack the year before where nine colleagues tragically lost their lives and a further 40 were injured, this being the incident with the highest loss of life for the RUC. She states only since becoming a mother has she understood fully how her own mother felt when she was told of the posting.

There she was met by a female station sergeant, this was really encouraging to see - not only another female officer but one in the rank of sergeant. There was generally only one female per section and many areas didn't have female officers at all. There were also a large number of military officers, compounding the male dominated environment. Forkhill and Crossmaglen, where officers had to stay over for a number of nights, had no accommodation for female officers and she would have been flown in to patrol with her male colleagues. Bearing in mind at this point that male officers in Northern Ireland were armed but female officers were not (and would not be until early 1994[173]). Michele recalls on her third night duty, her team were tasked to a traveller site to make an arrest. She was told to stay in the car, in the backseat, and given the rifle to look after - she had no idea what to do with it! Suddenly the door opened and a prisoner was placed in the car beside her and she was told to "keep an eye on him". For a 19 year old officer, who had no experience of firearms, now with a violent prisoner, the experience was terrifying and Michele remembers it clearly.

Two years into the job, on her first day in CID, both of Michele's senior officers were tragically ambushed and killed. The very next day a 19 year old civilian was killed in an explosion at Warrenpoint Police Station. She

246 | P a g e

recalls the fast pace of the incident rooms and sombre mood that prevailed. Those were dark days and she acknowledges the progress achieved in Northern Ireland since then. She remembers strong comradeship and her male colleagues really appreciated female support, especially with things like searching female prisoners or female associates of male offenders who would seek to move weapons by hiding them in prams or shopping. Female officers were absolutely operationally crucial in this respect, often diffusing tensions where conflict would flare up and also in endeavouring to establish trust with families and communities not supportive of policing in Northern Ireland at this time. The increase of females also supported the evolution of better practices, especially for victims of sexual offences and domestic abuse.

From the very beginning, Michele was very clear about her values and what was acceptable to be said or done, in the spirit of 'police banter'. She feels this contributed to the fact that she experienced less of colleagues being disrespectful or inappropriate.

As Michele progressed through the different ranks she recalls often, being accompanied by male colleagues, where the assumption was made by others the male was the lead or senior officer. This often stemmed from so few females holding positions of rank. The early experiences Michele encountered in policing has shaped her drive to deliver a tailored policing service which is very much focused on community needs. Michele's service is predominantly operational, holding firearms and public order command, along with a number of headquarters postings. She believes she has benefitted from fantastic opportunities in policing, having attended the FBI Academy twice, attachments to New York and Washington police departments, delivered a community policing project in Mongolia through the Constitutional and Legal Policy Institute in Budapest and lectured at Guelph University in Toronto on community policing in a divided society.

She has experienced many changes in policing, including the transition from RUCGC to PSNI, through the Independent Review of Policing (Patten recommendations). Michele's highlight was her success at the Police National Assessment Centre in December 2014 and graduating from the Strategic Command Course, only the second female in Northern Ireland to do so. Her attendance on this national leadership programme led to Michele making her biggest decision in policing, to leave Northern Ireland. Attracted by the policing challenge of the second largest police force in England, their approach and significant change programme being designed, she joined West Midlands Police.

In doing so, she became the first female officer in a substantive executive rank post in West Midlands Police to have children. She has first-hand experience of the challenges in juggling her work and personal life, making the tough decision to move to Birmingham for work and commuting home to her husband and children in Northern Ireland on a weekly basis.

Michele is the Assistant Chief Constable for West Midlands Police with responsibility for local policing and the preventative approach. In the 2020 change programme, she leads on developing the next generation of local policing, involving citizens in policing, offender management and communicating with our communities digitally as well as through more traditional methods. She is also the regional lead on mental health issues and fast track officer development schemes.

Michele believes diversity remains a challenge for policing, not only in regard to women but in welcoming diversity in terms of race, religion, background and sexual orientation, as well as differences in personality, ways of working and thinking. Policing is still male dominated so support from male colleagues and their influence is vitally important. Role models, agile working and creating opportunities to allocate women into challenging areas of the business, in order to develop their skills and prepare them for stepping into more senior roles, are all important aspects of achieving parity in the workplace. She said:

'Diversity brings a greater range of skills and knowledge that we can use to solve problems and improve our service to a range of different communities and situations. It is also central to our legitimacy and assists us to build and maintain their public trust and confidence.' Michele retired in 2017 having completed 30 years' service.

Louisa Rolfe

Louisa's career started in Avon and Somerset Police, where she rose from being a Bristol response officer to becoming one of the country's most senior female officers. Louisa grew up in South Gloucestershire and joining the police service never entered her head until she visited a university careers fair. At school she enjoyed science but was always fascinated by psychology so she chose a degree course that combined her interest with a familiar subject she knew she enjoyed. She graduated from the University of Bristol with a Joint Honours Degree in Zoology and Psychology. She left knowing that science and academia were not for her but criminal psychology had captured her interest and she wanted a job that involved working with people. When she secured her police job, her parents remember her elderly grandfather, a very serious chap, laughing until he cried: Louisa was always the most mischievous of his grandchildren.

Louisa loved the challenge of policing from the moment she joined. She was a constable for seven years before securing a place on the Accelerated Promotion Course. This coincided with her passing her sergeants board and also starting CID training. She had to drop the CID training to start as a sergeant but kept a burning ambition to be a detective and, despite the pace of promotion on the APC scheme, she returned to detective posts at sergeant and inspector rank, finally securing a detective chief inspector job at Weston Super Mare in North Somerset. She reluctantly left this post when she was selected to be the Chief Constable's staff officer. Having not applied she resisted the move but recognises that this job gave her such valuable insight into senior leadership that it shaped her career from then on. Determined to get back to being a detective, Louisa secured promotion to detective superintendent in the Major Crime Investigation Team and eventually became Avon and Somerset's first woman head of CID but not before being wrenched away again to temporarily lead the Operations Department. Completely out of her comfort zone, Louisa learnt hugely important lessons about leadership in this role: 'I learnt that I cannot possibly know everything and that my team respect me more for admitting when I don't know and tapping in to their valuable expertise. Showing genuine interest in their work, valuing their expertise and caring about what is important to them counts for so much more'.

In her role as Head of CID she led on development of a Regional Organised Crime Unit and Counter Terrorism Intelligence Unit in the South West and a two-force Major Crime Investigation Team. Passionate about diversity and equality issues, Louisa helped increase the representation of women in senior detective posts across Avon and Somerset - 'When a senior colleague joined from another force he joked that I had created The Number One Ladies Detective Agency - like the novel.'

DCC Rolfe is also the National Police Chiefs' Council lead for domestic abuse. She led the UK police response to HMIC's report *Everyone's Business* – which focused on improving the response to domestic abuse survivors – urging forces to prioritise domestic abuse and securing substantial improvements across the service. Louisa recalls 'I was put forward for this national role by my then Chief Constable. It has sometimes been hard to juggle with the day job but I have learnt so much. I cannot control the way every force responds to domestic abuse but I have learnt how to influence more effectively and also be an advocate for the service. I firmly believe officers want to support victims of domestic abuse and achieve justice for them but it is not a straightforward crime. Officers deserve effective support, not only from senior officers but also partners like CPS and Social Care'.

Louisa joined West Midlands Police as Deputy Chief Constable in February 2016. Her role with the force is to oversee the force's WMP2020 change programme that features 33 individual projects designed to make the force more agile when fighting crime and more accessible to the public. She states 'Moving to a new force has been a huge challenge but very rewarding. I have felt welcome and supported and it is great to make a new start and think about how you make best use of all that you have learnt elsewhere. Moving my family away from their home and friends has been the hardest part but we are settled in the Midlands now.'

Current statistics

In August 2016[174] West Midlands Police reported that just over 30% of its police officers were female. This compares to just over 47% of the PCSO strength, a little over 17% of the special constables and just over 61% of the police staff workforce.

Of the officers on the force's Executive Team (NPCC rank officers of Assistant Chief Constable or higher) - one third are female, with a female Assistant Chief Constable and a female Deputy Chief Constable. NPCC rank is marginally the most diverse rank of West Midlands Police in terms of gender:

Rank	Females	Total	Percentage
Chief Superintendent	6	20	30.00%
Superintendent	9	29	31.03%
Chief Inspector	16	67	23.88%
Inspector	74	257	28.79%
Sergeant	211	886	23.81%
Constable	1702	5441	31.28%

2017 – 100 Years On

Officers have much more support nowadays than ever before, including childcare vouchers, flexible working options and wellbeing support.

Female officers are now represented in every operational department within West Midlands Police, including fast paced confrontational roles in departments such as the Operational Support Unit, Firearms Operations Unit and Response.

PC Maria McNeil and PC Georgina Oakley, response officers in Birmingham

Flexible working

Women account for a high percentage of workers on atypical or reduced hours contracts in the UK, where around a quarter of the workforce is part-time. Most people choose to work less hours than they could due to caring responsibilities for children or older relatives, although there is increasing evidence of demand in the workforce for agility. Indeed, recent research shows that the ability to work flexibly is favoured by many employees more than a pay rise!

The business benefits of flexible working are just as relevant at WMP as in any workplace – perhaps more so, where the demands on employees are rigorous, expectations high, and terms and conditions sometimes squeezed by austerity or politics about the pay and conditions of public sector workers. WMP has many measures in place in support of the organisation's ambition of being a family friendly employer, but interesting challenges reside in the balance between individual needs and the requirements of the organisation.

Flexible working can be an emotive issue, and while police officers can sometimes be found suitable alternative roles, it is not so simple to redeploy a member of staff due to the different employment framework that applies, and many of the employees in an organisation such as WMP are highly specialised. Where both partners, or co-carers, work for the organisation, there may be more scope to find a solution to amend working hours that meets the needs of the family involved and their teams, but it can also be a problem where the couple may work shift rotations that do not coincide or may clash. It could be said that more work is being done by fewer people, and the technology we now have to assist may not always bridge the gap between demand and resource to meet that need. Effort is often made by managers and HR staff to find solutions to flexible working challenges, as operational resilience is so much reduced. But it is not always easy.

So what is *flexible working*? A flexible working agreement is an arrangement between the organisation and the employee that involves a departure from conventional standard hours. Part time working is most common, but there are many other possibilities, such as compressed hours (full time hours worked over fewer days than normal), term time working (when the employee's pay and hours are calculated across school terms), job shares (where two employees effectively share one full time job equally between them) or annualised hours (the hours are calculated over a 12 month period, rather than fixed each day or week).

Under Part 8A of the Employment Rights Act 1996, employees have the right to request flexible working, which was extended in 2014 to all employees on completion of 26 weeks' service. The Flexible Working Regulations of 2002 were also then repealed, removing the strict statutory procedure for considering requests, and employers are now required to process requests in a 'reasonable manner, which is underpinned by an ACAS Code of Practice. In fact, WMP was ahead of that change and already operating in accordance with the code. WMP flexible working policy and guidance has been developed over the last 20 years and is frequently updated in pursuit of the force's ambition to be a modern, family-friendly employer, and to support managers considering requests.

It was not always thus. The contrast between the conditions under which employees, particularly females, have worked under in the police should not be underestimated. During the 1920s the lady enquiry officer in the CID had to be on call 24/7 to deal with enquiries regarding women or children and she worked alone (although cover was arranged from the Women Police Department for periods of annual leave). Female officers were sparse and had to work long hours and cover for each other if they were sick or on leave. Less than a century ago, officers also only got two days of leave every month.

More recently, the baby boomer generation of women discovered that policing and family life were often incompatible, and at that time very little statutory support existed, so female officers simply left at the point they married or found they were expecting. Female officers who took maternity leave as recently as the 1980s tell anecdotes about unnecessarily restricted duties patronisingly imposed on them when they reported their pregnancy, colleagues who smoked in close proximity to them in the workplace, and the detrimental impact on a career of taking time out to have a family. Eyebrow-raising now, but probably no more sexist than society was in general at the time.

Things have certainly moved on significantly, and of course equal pay legislation ensures that the jobs done by women are compensated appropriately. Inevitably though, biology makes a difference. The working women of today have greater opportunities and more choices, but their income and pensions are inevitably affected when they take time out for maternity leave, or reduce their working hours, even though they are very much supported to maintain their careers within WMP.

Carers, defined as *'anyone who cares, unpaid, for a friend or family member who due to illness, disability, a mental health problem or an addiction cannot cope without their support'*, are employees whose needs may be less predictable than parents, but who similarly require some flexibility to support their, usually adult, dependents. WMP undertook a forcewide survey of carers needs in 2014, and the responses indicated that over 70% of them work full time, but many struggle. On the basis of feedback received, two thirds of WMP's carers are women. Once again, managerial empathy and flexibility was a big issue.

Each generation of women in WMP helps the organisation learn and adapt, to improving its approach. WMP now employs men and women at all levels who work flexibly, some who even live elsewhere and interrupt their working week to spend time at home. Increasingly, the ability to work a non-conventional pattern, or from a variety of locations, is an issue that affects whether candidates choose to accept a job at WMP.

New recruits

New recruits going through their training at the start of 2017, who originally applied in 2015, consist of 146 female officers (37% of total intake) from 1,033 females (31% of total) who applied. The female candidates could be considered on the whole as being more successful than the male candidates, as their percentage of the whole increased, whereas the male percentage decreased through the recruitment process. Two of the stories of the latest intake of new recruits are detailed below:

Kat Weir

Although her father worked for Warwickshire Police, Kat originally wanted to be a barrister. She was completing her UCAS form to confirm exactly what she wanted to undertake at university when she had a last minute change of mind and decided to do English. She ended up meeting someone at university who wanted to be a police officer who sold it to her so much she decided to do that instead.

Kat graduated from Oxford Brookes University with a 2:1 in English Language in 2013. She became a Police Community Support Officer (PCSO) in Thames Valley Police in 2014. She really enjoyed this role until the policy on what PCSOs could deal with changed and her work ended up mainly consisting of non-crime and mental health jobs. She found this really frustrating, mainly because she felt that she was not equipped to deal with mental health but also because she wanted to be more involved in other areas of policing.

Her work as a PCSO gave her experience of community engagement and building relationships with the public, but it frustrated Kat how limited the role became. She felt she was perfectly capable of doing the role of an officer so in early 2015 she put her application in to West

Midlands Police and subsequently started her training in September 2016. She turned 25 in October 2016.

Kat is particularly interested in progressing a career either as a dog handler or a traffic officer. She states she has been absolutely baffled by the kind of things people call the police for, personally she would never have considered calling the police except in emergency.

One particular question during her interview has stayed in Kat's mind: 'How are you going to cope in a male dominated world?' This caught her off guard because she felt it to be untrue. She states the gender of her colleagues has never crossed her mind, she feels like everyone is equal and she doesn't normally notice the male/female split. Everyone is there to do a job and she doesn't notice if she is surrounded by male officers. Kat states 'The service feels very equal and I haven't experienced discrimination or gender inequality.'

Kat would be interested in eventually progressing to the rank of inspector but would like to know more about the role played by different ranks. She is full of optimism about the future of female officers in the police service and almost feels like the topic is a moot point.

Gail Arnold

Gail joined the force a lot later than most of the officers in her recruitment cohort. She has already had 30 years work experience outside of policing, which she feels will stand her in good stead when she goes out to jobs in the future.

She states she always wanted to be a police officer and first applied back in 1984. She got through to interview but one question in particular threw her off: 'Why should we employ a woman as a police officer? Is a woman going to be effective in a riot situation when there are big strong men?' An 18-year-old Gail did not know how to answer this question at all. Now she appreciates how a female officer would try and talk down the situation before it escalates and she states being a mother to two teenage boys has certainly given her a lot of experience in this area!

After failing at her initial attempt to join the police, Gail started her working life in banking. She recalls going for a promotion when she was 18 and her manager said to her 'Why should we promote you when there are men we could promote? After all you will be pushing a pram down the high street in five years' time.'

Now Gail feels that women are all treated exactly the same as men, inside and outside policing. After spending over two decades in banking, she worked for two years in the control room of West Midlands Fire Service and witnessed the increase in female fire fighters there.

It is true that equality in policing has come a long way in a relatively short space of time. Considering that female police officers have existed for 100 years, the past two or three decades have seen women bridge the gap in leaps and bounds. Officers with 20+ years' service now recall a very different working environment and Gail has had very different experiences from those of young female police officers today. She does feel though that it is a reflection of the evolvement of society as a whole, not just policing.

During the last 30 years Gail has been married twice, divorced once and raised a girl and two boys. She states she has never stopped wanting to have another go at joining the police but she had her family to consider and then when she finally did feel ready recruitment had stopped.

At the start of 2015 she saw that recruitment had finally reopened. At age 48, she decided to go for it and was successful.

Gail is visibly excited to be here and finally realise her dream. She states she has been treated the same as everyone else, even though the rest of her cohort are on average 30 years younger. She hasn't personally seen any evidence of discrimination. She feels her life experience will be really valuable and help her to address different situations. Now she is comfortable to sit back, listen and gather information to help her make decisions, compared to her 18 year old self where she was young, naïve and eager to prove herself.

Gail says 'It's never too late to achieve your dreams and I am evidence of that'.

Police Now

Police Now is an initiative aimed at attracting graduates into a career in policing. In August 2015 the Metropolitan Police Service decided to establish Police Now as an independent charity. It is able to qualify as a charity given the explicit 'not-for-profit' arrangements and their stated intent to make a contribution to policing and a difference in those communities that need it most. The Police Transformation Fund awarded £5,331,584 for Police Now to be paid, in mainly quarterly instalments, across two financial years (2016/17: £1.8m and 2017/18: £3.5m).

In its first year Police Now was piloted by the Metropolitan Police Service. In 2016 the programme expanded to seven forces, and by 2017 it will include almost half of all police forces across the country.

In July 2016 West Midlands Police joined the scheme with 14 candidates - four female and 10 male. One of the females did not complete the summer academy however she has joined a regular intake of officers in the force since. These statistics do not reflect the national picture however as the 2016 intake across all forces was in fact 53% female. The quality of candidates is very high and interest considerable. The successful candidates have a two year contract and are given neighbourhood policing roles in high crime areas with a chance for them to try out new ideas to solve policing problems in that area. On completion of the two years, the recruits can continue in their neighbourhood role, transfer to another officer role or move beyond policing.

The training was delivered by the Police Now programme in London. This started on 18th July 2016 and ran for six weeks, known as the summer academy. It was an intense training programme, with recruits learning for 11 hours each day. There were additional demands including a weekend and evenings to ensure they passed the rigorous testing. They would also be out "on Borough" during the training so that they had operational hands on experience.

PC Alexandra Paxton & PC Sinead Cleaver, officers from the first intake of WMP Police Now officers

Closing Statement

I have thought about what advice I might offer to women joining the service now. It would be to consider every challenge as an opportunity.

Policing can be a hard slog but it is also incredibly rewarding. It keeps your feet on the ground and makes you thankful for what you have. If something stretches you and even scares you a little, you are likely to learn and grow from the experience. Also, don't restrict your ambition or aspirations.

Be determined if you know what you want. I was told by well-meaning colleagues when I joined the service that promotion opportunities were limited so I was wasting my time thinking beyond inspector. I was also told that I couldn't be a senior detective unless I had been a career detective. Proving them wrong hasn't been easy but I've had a great time.

We have so much to be thankful to the pioneer policewomen for, those who took the first steps, those who held the first positions in each rank and those who braved male dominated environments to undertake specialist roles.

The police service has come such a long way over the past 100 years and it is exciting to be part of the journey going forwards.

Deputy Chief Constable Louisa Rolfe

Female Firsts in Policing in the West Midlands

Evelyn Miles and Rebecca Lipscombe – 1917, Birmingham's first female police officers

First female special constables in the country, in Wolverhampton 1917:

Hilda Hutchinson Smith	Lillie Highfield-Jones M.B.E.	Carmen Buchanan
Sylvia May Sankey	Muriel Elsie Hobbs	Elsie Leonora Corbett
Lilian Manley	Gertrude Buxton Matthews	Doris M. Mulliner
Florence I. Manley	Lizzie Brookes	Catherine B. Thomson
Sarah A. Tonks	Jane Buckley	Elizabeth Shingler
Lilian Humphreys	Ida Robinson	Susan Parker
May Nickless	Agnes Eason	Phillis Killin
Kathleen Smith	Doris Higgs	Mary Hanmer
Gladys M. Hill	Janet Killin	Dorothy Sargent
Amy E. Lockwood		

Evelyn Miles – 1918, Birmingham's first female sergeant

Katherine Tearle and Miss Williams – 1918, Walsall's first female officers

Katherine Tearle – 1919, Walsall's first female sergeant

Susan Florence Palmer and Mildred Florence White – 1930, Birmingham's first female inspectors

Hannah Esther Bronwen Evans – 1937, Wolverhampton's first female officer

Ena Goodacre and Kathleen Rowe – 1938, Coventy's first female officers

Ena Goodacre – 1943, Coventry's first sergeant

Agnes Rooss and Doreen Carter – 1947, Dudley's first female officers

First Birmingham Police female special constables in 1949:

Name	Age	Occupation	Divisional number
Margaret Delaney	38 yrs	Shorthand typist	W1
Joyce Clarke	29yrs	Shorthand typist	W2
Marjorie Lewis	31yrs	Shorthand typist	W3
Bessie Thomas	33yrs	Shorthand typist	W4
Jean Varley	26yrs	Shorthand typist	W5
Marjorie Begett	36yrs	Secretary	W6
Betty Chamberlain	28yrs	Shorthand typist	W7
Lilian Haddock	32yrs	Shorthand typist	W8
Hilda Gidney	28yrs	Shorthand typist	W9
Hilda Hammond	38yrs	u/k	W10
Vera Haill	29yrs	Clerk typist	W11
Marie Lea	31yrs	Shorthand typist	W12

Norah Gray – 1950 and 1954, Birmingham's first female chief inspector and superintendent

Doreen Carter – 1955, Dudley's first female sergeant

Angela Harwood – 1959, Birmingham's first female cadet

Kathleen Crocker – 1963, Walsall's first female inspector

Pauline Elsie Wren – 1974, first female chief superintendent in the West Midlands

Pauline Campbell-Moss – 1974, first black female officer in the West Midlands

Christine Read – 1978, first female patrol motorcyclist in the West Midlands

Elizabeth Dodd – 1979, first female dog handler in the West Midlands

Angie Clamp – 1984, first female diver in the West Midlands

Kay Weale – 1985, first female mounted officer in West Midlands Police

Shindo Barquer – 1987, first female Sikh officer in the West Midlands

Liz Crawley – 1990, first female driving instructor in the West Midlands

Kerry Delaney – 1990 - first female OSU officer in the West Midlands

Julia Walsh – 1991, first black female sergeant in the West Midlands

Sarah Walker – 1998, first female officer in Air Ops in the West Midlands

Ashley Moore – 2000, first female firearms officer attached to an Armed Response Vehicle

Pat Barnett – 1991, as acting Assistant Chief Constable became first female to hold the rank in West Midlands

Anne Summers – 1996 and 1999, first substantive female Assistant Chief Constable and later Deputy Chief Constable in the West Midlands

BIRMINGHAM CITY POLICE.

CONDITIONS OF SERVICE TO BE SIGNED BY A POLICE
------------ WOMAN ON APPOINTMENT. ------------

1. Each Policewoman will be enrolled for one year on probation, and if then recommended by the Chief Constable as fit, may be appointed by the Watch Committee. A Policewoman on probation may be dismissed by the Chief Constable for unfitness, negligence or misconduct, and her services may be dispensed with if she is inefficient in the performance of her work.

2. A Policewoman shall devote her whole time to the Police Service of the City. She must not, directly or indirectly, carry on any trade or calling; nor can she be permitted, without the consent of the Chief Constable to live at any place where any member of her family carries on business.

3. She shall serve where appointed, and reside in the City, and within a reasonable distance of the Station to which she may be attached, unless otherwise permitted by the Chief Constable.

4. She shall not, directly or indirectly, be interested in any public house or beerhouse. She is prohibited from borrowing money from publicans, beerhouse keepers, or other tradesmen, or being in any way indebted to them. She may not reside in a house licensed for the sale of intoxicating liquors.

5. She shall conform to all rules, regulations, fines and deductions now in force, or as the Watch Committee may frame, for preventing any neglect or abuse, and making the City Police efficient in the discharge of their duties, and shall promptly obey all the orders of the Chief Constable, and others placed in authority over her.

6. She shall appear in her complete Police Uniform at all times when required, but she may wear plain clothes when off duty.

7. She shall at all times provide herself with a respectable suit of plain clothes.

8. Single women on joining will not be permitted to marry until they have been in the force one year, and received permission of the Chief Constable.

9. In the event of a Policewoman marrying, the Police Authority reserve to themselves the right to decide whether she shall remain in the Police Force or otherwise.

10. In the event of pregnancy the condition shall be reported without delay to the Chief Constable, and she may be required to resign from the Police Force at the discretion of the Police Authority. Re-admission to the Police Force will also be subject to their discretion.

11. Such debts owing by her as the Watch Committee or Chief Constable directs to be paid shall be paid by her forthwith.

12. She shall not belong to or subscribe money to the funds of any political or party society.

13. She shall have no claim to any stolen or unclaimed money or property, or other money or property found by her, or that may have come into her possession in the execution of her duty, and she shall deliver up all such money and property to her Superintendent; to be accounted for in accordance with the regulations relating to lost or stolen property.

continued..............

14. She shall not retain any money or other thing given to her by
way of fee, reward, or presentation, without permission of the
Watch Committee on the recommendation of the Chief Constable.

15. Her pension will be in accordance with the Police Pensions Act
1921 and will be calculated upon the amount of her pay, from
which a deduction of 5 per cent is made for superannuation, and
not on the amount of any extra pay or allowance she may receive.

16. She will be entitled to free medical attendance whilst serving as
laid down in the Police Regulations, but she will not be entitled
to pay if absent from duty without leave.

17. She will make written application for promotion from one class to
another, when promotion falls due; otherwise her promotion may
be delayed; and the Watch Committee reserve the right to defer
payment or to reduce her pay for misconduct or inefficiency.

18. She will be required to pass an educational test before receiving
her first promotion, and may be called on for similar tests as to
efficiency before further promotion.

19. She will be required to obtain first, second and third class
St. John Ambulance Certificates within three years of her joining
the Force, and to attend revision class each year subsequently
to keep up her efficiency in rendering "First Aid" to the injured.

20. She shall not resign or withdraw herself from her duties or from
the Force unless allowed to do so in writing by the Chief Constable
or unless she shall have given to the Chief Constable one month's
previous notice in writing, at the same time assigning a reason
for so doing. If she resign or withdraw such leave or notice
she is liable to forfeit all pay and allowances due.

21. She is liable to immediate dismissal for unfitness, negligence,
or misconduct, independently of any other punishment to which,
by law, she may be subject. The Watch Committee may remove her
from the service by dismissal, or otherwise punish her for misconduct.

22. A Policewoman may also be required to resign on account of
undesirable conduct on the part of her husband.

23. A Policewoman dismissed from the Police Force, or who resigns,
or ceases to hold office, shall forthwith deliver up all articles
of clothing, accoutrements, appointments, and other necessaries
that have been supplied to her for the execution of her duties.
They do not become her property, and she shall also deliver them
up whenever called upon to do so complete, and in good order.
If such clothing or appointments have in the opinion of the Chief
Constable been unduly worn or improperly used or damaged, a
deduction from the pay then due to the policewoman shall be made,
sufficient to make good the damage or supply a new article.

24. Her normal daily period of duty will be 8 hours, to be performed
as directed.

25. She will be given one day's rest in seven, and she will be granted
Annual Leave as prescribed by the Police Regulations.

CONDITIONS OF SERVICE OF POLICEWOMEN

The main conditions of service in the Police are governed by the Police Acts and the Police Regulations made by the Secretary of State under Section 33 of the Police Act, 1964, and by the Police Pensions Act, 1948, and the Police Pensions Regulations. The following paragraphs contain the more important conditions for the time being in force, stated in general terms for the guidance of candidates, and certain other conditions which every candidate must accept on appointment.

1.—PAY. The scale for women constables is £630 a year on appointment, rising after one year to £655 and thereafter by one annual increment of £65, one of £25, one of £35, two of £30, one of £35, and a further two of £30, rising to £935 after nine years' service. In addition, a woman constable receives supplementary payments of £30 a year on completion of 17 years' service, and £30 a year on completion of 22 years' service, giving a final maximum of £995 a year.

There is also a special entry scale for women constables appointed at age 22 and above. This scale is £720 a year on appointment, rising after two years to £745, and after four years to £780, after which the normal scale will apply.

The scale for women Sergeants is £1,055 a year, rising by two annual increments of £35 and £40 respectively to £1,130 a year.

2.—PROMOTION. Appointments above the rank of constable in the women police are filled from within the Police Service. It is one of the conditions for promotion to Sergeant or Inspector that qualifying examinations in Police and educational subjects shall have been passed. Officers passing the qualifying examinations appropriate to the ranks of Constable and Sergeant receive a once-for-all allowance of £30 in each rank. No qualifying examinations are set for promotion to the ranks above Inspector. Wide opportunities of advancement exist, which may be gained by good conduct, intelligence and application to duty.

3.—PENSION CONTRIBUTIONS. Under the Police Pensions Regulations, new entrants are required to pay pension contributions to the Police Authority at the rate of 4½% of pay less 1/2d. per week.

4.—PENSIONS. An ordinary pension is granted on retirement any time after completing 25 years' pensionable service. The rate of pension ranges from half pay on retirement after 25 years' pensionable service up to two thirds of pay on retirement after 30 years' pensionable service or more. Pay for this purpose being averaged over the last three years of service. For a new entrant an ordinary pension awarded upon less than 30 years' pensionable service does not come into payment unless, or until, the pensioner is 50 years old. Up to one quarter of a pension awarded after not less than 30 years' service may be commuted for a lump sum.

A Policewoman who is permanently disabled as a result of an injury or disease received in the execution of her duty without her own default is granted an ill-health pension, and if the aggregate of this and certain National Insurance benefits to which she may be entitled is less than a specified amount, depending on her length of service and degree of disablement, she is granted a supplemental pension to bring the aggregate up to the specified amount. Up to one quarter of an ill-health pension, (but not a supplemental pension) may be commuted for a lump sum.

A policewoman who retires on medical grounds in other circumstances is granted an ill-health pension if she has completed ten years' pensionable service. If she has not completed ten years' pensionable service she is granted a gratuity.

Children's allowances may be payable in certain circumstances following the death of a policewoman. Where death is the result of an attack or an injury received in effecting an arrest or preventing an escape, and the policewoman was the only surviving parent, the children may be granted a lump sum award.

Policewomen come within the flat-rate National Insurance Scheme in the same way as other employed people, and pay Class I contributions. It is on account of this that their contributions to the Police Pensions Scheme are reduced by 1/2d. per week and at National Insurance Retirement age (usually 60) their police pensions are reduced by an amount depending upon their years of service. The maximum reduction corresponding to 30 years' service is 19/6 a week. The Police Service has been contracted out of the graduated National Insurance scheme, however, and so the additional graduated National Insurance contributions are not paid by Police Officers, and graduated scheme pension benefits are not earned during police service; and police pensions are not normally further reduced at National Insurance retirement age on account of graduated scheme benefit.

5.—COMPULSORY RETIREMENT. Constables and Sergeants are required to retire on reaching the age of 55, but the compulsory retirement may be postponed by not more than 5 years by the Chief Officer of Police. Higher ages of compulsory retirement apply to some of the higher ranks. Up to one quarter of a pension awarded on retirement on age grounds may be commuted for a lump sum.

6.—HOURS OF DUTY. The normal period of duty is 88 hours a fortnight, performed in 11 daily periods of 8 hours. The Police Regulations prescribe conditions for the grant of compensation when overtime is worked.

7. —**LEAVE OF ABSENCE.** All ranks below Superintendent are entitled to seven rest days in each period of four weeks; to leave on, or compensation in lieu of, public holidays; and to annual leave on full pay as follows:—

Rank.		Leave.						
Constable	...	16 days (increasing to 18 days after 10 years' service).						
Sergeant	...	18 days (	,,	,, 20	,,	,, ,, ,,	,,	).
Inspector	...	21 days (	,,	,, 23	,,	,, ,, ,,	,,	).
Chief Inspector		24 days (	,,	,, 26	,,	,, ,, ,,	,,	).

All ranks receive full Police pay during absence from duty through sickness or injury, but from this is deducted the amount of any National Insurance sickness or injury benefit to which they may be entitled.

8.—**MARRIAGE.** Married women may be admitted as regular members of Police Forces and an unmarried constable who marries after she joins is not compelled to resign on that account. Under the provisions of the Police Regulations married policewomen are entitled to maternity leave in part on full pay and for the remainder without pay.

9.—**ACCOMMODATION.** Free quarters are provided by the Police Authority or a rent allowance is granted in lieu. Income Tax paid on a rent allowance is re-imbursed.

10.—**REMOVALS.** Where a member of the Police Force is required to move her home in consequence of a transfer to another part of the police area, her removal expenses are re-imbursed and an allowance is payable in respect of reasonable expenditure incidental to the move.

11.—**UNIFORM and EQUIPMENT.** All articles of uniform clothing and equipment necessary for the performance of police duty are provided by the Police Authority free of cost; such articles do not become the property of the individual members of the force and must be delivered up on leaving the Force.

12.—A Constable is on probation for a period of two years. During this period her services may be dispensed with at any time if the Chief Officer of Police considers that she is not fitted to perform the duties of her office. A Constable whose services are so dispensed with is entitled to receive one month's notice or one month's pay in lieu thereof, and to the return of her pension contributions.

13.—No person shall be eligible for appointment to a Police Force and the services of a woman member of a Police Force may be dispensed with at any time if, without the consent of the Chief Officer of Police:—

(a) she carries on any business or holds any office or employment for hire or gain, or

(b) she resides at any premises where her husband or any member of her family keeps a shop or carries on any like business, or

(c) she holds, or her husband or any member of her family living with her holds, any licence granted in pursuance of the liquor licensing laws, or the laws regulating places of public entertainment in the area of the police force in which she seeks appointment or to which she has been appointed, as the case may be, or has any pecuniary interest in such licence, or

(d) her husband not being separated or divorced from her, keeps a shop or carries on any like business in the area of the police force in which she seeks appointment, or to which she has been appointed, as the case may be.

14.—A Constable becomes, on appointment, a member of the Police Federation instituted under the Police Acts. She must not be a member of any outside Association having for its object, or one of its objects to control or influence the pay or other conditions of service of the Police, and she must not, save in special circumstances with the consent of the Chief Officer of Police, be a member of any Trade Union. (Note: A breach of this condition disqualifies a constable from membership of a Police Force).

15.—Every Constable must devote her whole time to the Police Service. She must attend at any time to any matter which arises within the scope of her duty as a constable, and must promptly obey all lawful orders of the persons in authority over her.

16.—A Constable must serve wherever she is ordered and her place of residence is subject to the approval of the Chief Officer of Police.

17.—Where a constable occupies a house provided by the Police Authority she must not, without the previous consent of the Chief Officer of Police receive a lodger or sub-let a part of the house. In any other case a constable must notify the Chief Officer of Police of her intention to receive a lodger or sub-let a part of the house.

18.—A constable must not without the previous consent of the Chief Officer of Police, accept or receive directly or indirectly from any person, any money, reward or present, or any valuable consideration whatever on account of anything done by her as a constable.

19.—A constable must promptly discharge all lawful debts, and in case of failure to do so, must report the circumstances to the Chief Officer of Police.

20.—A constable must avoid, whether on duty or in private life any conduct or behaviour likely to bring discredit on the Police Service. She must also abstain from any activities calculated to interfere with the impartial discharge of her duties, and, in particular, she must not take any active part in politics.

21.—A constable must not resign or withdraw herself from duty except after giving one month's notice in writing, or such shorter notice as the Police Authority may accept.

22.—A constable must not enter a public house in uniform without permission, except in the execution of her duty.

A BREACH OF ANY OF CONDITIONS 15 TO 22 CONSTITUTES AN OFFENCE AGAINST
DISCIPLINE AND RENDERS A CONSTABLE LIABLE TO PUNISHMENT.

With Thanks

Debbie Menzel, West Midlands Police Museum

Su and Paul Handford, West Midlands Police Museum

Tony Rose, West Midlands Police Museum

Kay Weale

Liz Sumner (nee Crawley)

Kerry Delaney

Angie Clamp

Sarah Hipkins (nee Walker)

Ashley Moore (nee Powell)

Julia Walsh

Anne Summers

ACC Michele Larmour, West Midlands Police

DCC Louisa Rolfe, West Midlands Police

Chief Constable Suzette Davenport, Gloucestershire Police

Sharon Rowe

Kat Weir

Gail Arnold

Joan Lock for her support and use of her image of Mary Allen and Margaret Damer-Dawson

Library of Birmingham for use of their image of Alderman Sayer and facilitating access to records

Linda Fraser

Malcolm Fraser

Doreen and Conrad Joseph, former Walsall officers

Eileen Robinson, for the story of Catherine (Kate) Downey

The Birmingham History Forum

Gary Stack, West Midlands Police

Ade Ford, West Midlands Police

Becky Hess

Chief Superintendent Sally Bourner, West Midlands Police

Sharon Fountain, West Midlands Police

Graham Bedingfield, West Midlands Police

The Metropolitan Women Police Association and the Met Heritage Centre

Helen Kirkman, for historic research

The Devil's Porridge Museum

Paul Lines, Mapseeker Publishing

Anne Malpass and Wendy Robinson, Kathleen Rowe's daughters

Jill Page, Hannah Esther Bronwen Evans' daughter

List of Pictures

1) Front page - picture of a sign originating from Brierley Hill Police Station, West Midlands Police Museum (and yes we know there is a spelling error!)
2) Corinne Brazier and Steve Rice, West Midlands Police
3) Chief Constable Dave Thompson QPM LLB, West Midlands Police
4) Mary Allen and Margaret Damer-Dawson: https://en.wikipedia.org/wiki/Mary_Sophia_Allen#/media/File:Women_at_work_during_the_First_World_War_Q108495.jpg
5) King George V and Princess Mary inspecting the munitions police at Gretna, 1917, courtesy of the Devil's Porridge Museum
6) Mary Allen and Margaret Damer-Dawson, photo courtesy of Joan Lock
7) Dorothy Peto, Director of the Bristol Training School, from a post card in Dorothy Peto's personal file
8) Charles Haughton Rafter, from a painting in the West Midlands Police Museum collection
9) Evelyn Miles and Rebecca Lipscombe from the Birmingham Weekly Mercury 9th June 1917, image re-printed with permission from Mirrorpix
10) Wolverhampton Female Specials, Wolverhamptonswar.wordpress courtesy of Wolverhampton City Archives
11) Sergeant Tearle and Miss Williams, 1916-1917 Women Police Service report, Metropolitan Women Police Association, Met Heritage Centre
12) Lady Nancy Astor, first female Member of Parliament to sit in Westminster, https://en.wikipedia.org/wiki/Nancy_Astor,_Viscountess_Astor#/media/File:Nancy_Astor.jpg accessed 8/12/2016
13) Constance Markievicz, historytoday.com 'Soldiers Are We': Women in the Irish Rising The en:Countess Markiewicz (1887-1927). Photography: Getty / Hulton
14) Policewomen c1919, West Midlands Police Museum
15) Two unconfirmed women from 1919 picture, West Midlands Police Museum
16) Evelyn Miles, West Midlands Police Museum
17) Evelyn Miles, West Midlands Police Museum
18) Lucy Charlton, West Midlands Police Museum
19) Ellen Vernon, West Midlands Police Museum
20) Ellen Vernon's uniform, West Midlands Police Museum
21) Sarah Hancox, West Midlands Police Museum
22) Catherine Downey, West Midlands Police
23) Catherine Downey, West Midlands Police

24) Catherine Downey and Ellen Vernon, West Midlands Police Museum
25) Adelaide Pearce, West Midlands Police
26) Alderman Sayer, reproduced with the permission of the Library of Birmingham
27) Chief Superintendent James Burnett, West Midlands Police Museum
28) Map showing proximity of Newton Street Police HQ and 67 Dale End, the hostel
29) Birmingham Police Aided Association post card, West Midlands Police Museum
30) Birmingham Police Aided Association shoe collection box, West Midlands Police Museum
31) Two images of Dorothy Peto, courtesy of Metropolitan Police Heritage Centre
32) Florence Mildred White, West Midlands Police Museum
33) Attested and cancelled – exert from file of Lucy Charlton, West Midlands Police Museum
34) Steelhouse Lane Police Station, by Steve Rice and Corinne Brazier
35) Steelhouse Lane Plaque, by Steve Rice & Corinne Brazier
36) Women Police c1935, from West Midlands Police Beacon magazine in 1980
37) Women Police 1936, West Midlands Police Museum
38) Hannah Esther Bronwen Evans, with thanks to her daughter Jill Page
39) Ena Goodacre, Coventry Evening Telegraph, 16th December 1943
40) Kathleen Rowe, My Weekly June 1996, with thanks to her daughters Wendy Robinson and Anne Malpass
41) Kathleen Rowe, from Wendy Robinson and Anne Malpass
42) Coventry officers group pic, from Wendy Robinson and Anne Malpass
43) Doreen Carter, West Midlands Police Museum
44) Susan Palmer, West Midlands Police Museum
45) Bessie Hale, West Midlands Police Museum
46) Agnes Ross, West Midlands Police Museum
47) Letter from Mrs Munton's file, West Midlands Police Museum
48) Doris Bushnell, West Midlands Police Museum
49) Young Norah Gray, West Midlands Police Museum
50) Older Norah Gray, West Midlands Police Museum
51) Norah Gray's application form, West Midlands Police Museum
52) Margaret MacRae, West Midlands Police Museum
53) Lock-up matron Miss Yates, West Midlands Police Museum

54) Bomb damaged Coventry Central Police Station, from Alamy.com
55) Old Coventry Police Station today, Steve Rice and Corinne Brazier
56) Tin police helmet, West Midlands Police Museum
57) Bomb damaged Newton Street, West Midlands Police Musuem.
58) Bomb damaged police HQ, West Midlands Police Museum
59) Old police HQ building now, Steve Rice and Corinne Brazier
60) Newton Street then – West Midlands Police Museum
61) Newton Street now - Steve Rice and Corinne Brazier
62) Newton Street police HQ – women going in, West Midlands Police Museum
63) Women's Auxiliary Police in Digbeth, West Midlands Police Museum
64) Women's Auxiliary Police superimposed onto Digbeth rear yard today, ©Graham Bedingfield
65) Females attending self-defence training in Digbeth Gym, West Midlands Police Museum
66) WAPC Marjorie Lewis, West Midlands Police Museum
67) WAPC gas mask training, West Midlands Police
68) WAPC Ada Wesley, West Midlands Police Museum
69) WAPC Jean Neill, West Midlands Police Museum
70) Victory parade led by Women Police and WAPC, West Midlands Police Museum
71) Reports from Evelyn Miles' report book, West Midlands Police Museum
72) Jeanie Law's application form, West Midlands Police Museum
73) Birmingham Policewomen c1940s, West Midlands Police Museum
74) Birmingham Policewomen c1940s (Sgt Schipper on left), West Midlands Police Museum
75) Agnes Tantrum, West Midlands Police Museum
76) Policewomen in Birmingham, West Midlands Police Museum
77) Ivy Dugard, West Midlands Police Museum
78) Alice Turner, West Midlands Police Museum
79) Female officer on traffic control, West Midlands Police Museum
80) Birmingham Policewomen, c1950s, West Midlands Police Museum
81) Jeanie Law, West Midlands Police Museum
82) WMP Women's Hockey Team 1998, West Midlands Police Museum
83) Mary Baldwin, West Midlands Police Museum
84) Young Florence Schipper, West Midlands Police Museum
85) Older Florence Schipper, West Midlands Police Museum
86) Young Helen Beattie, West Midlands Police Museum

87) Older Helen Beattie, West Midlands Police Museum
88) Kathleen Crocker, West Midlands Police Museum
89) Joan Langford, West Midlands Police Museum
90) Pauline Wren, West Midlands Police Museum
91) Barbara de Vitre, West Midlands Police Museum
92) Cadets at Tally Ho, West Midlands Police Museum
93) Cadets on drill at Tally Ho, West Midlands Police Museum
94) Angela Mary Harwood, West Midlands Police Museum
95) Angela Mary Harwood QSM, http://www.police.govt.nz/angela-harwood-qsm
96) Su Handford as a cadet, from Su Handford
97) Su Handford receiving the QPM, from Su Handford
98) Superintendent Evelyn Unett, West Midlands Police Museum
99) Doreen and Conrad Joseph – Walsall Police, from Doreen and Conrad Joseph
100) Doreen and Conrad Joseph, West Midlands Police
101) Birmingham City Police postcard, from Steve Rice
102) Pauline Campbell-Moss, from Pauline Campbell-Moss
103) Christine Read, West Midlands Police Museum
104) Liz Dodd, West Midlands Police Museum
105) Liz Dodd, West Midlands Police Museum
106) Angie Clamp, West Midlands Police Museum
107) Angie Clamp, West Midlands Police Museum
108) Kay Weale, West Midlands Police Museum
109) Kay Weale, West Midlands Police Museum
110) Liz Crawley, West Midlands Police Museum
111) Liz Crawley, West Midlands Police Museum
112) Kerry Delaney, Karen Audley and Linda Boyle, West Midlands Police Museum
113) Julia Walsh, West Midlands Police
114) Julia Walsh, West Midlands Police
115) Vanessa Carrol, West Midlands Police
116) Vanessa Carrol, West Midlands Police Museum
117) Anne Summers, West Midlands Police
118) Anne Summers, from Anne Summers
119) Sarah Walker, West Midlands Police Museum
120) Ashley Moore, from Ashley Moore
121) Ashley Moore, from Ashley Moore

122)	Deborah Harman-Burton, West Midlands Police
123)	Suzette Davenport, West Midlands Police
124)	Suzette Davenport, from Suzette Davenport
125)	Sharon Rowe, from Sharon Rowe
126)	Sharon Rowe, West Midlands Police
127)	Sally Bourner, aged 4, from Sally Bourner
128)	Sally Bourner, from Sally Bourner
129)	Sally Bourner, from Sally Bourner
130)	Female senior leaders in West Midlands Police: http://www.westmidlands-pcc.gov.uk/transparency/bob-jones-archive/2014-bob-jones-news-archive/women-lead-the-way-in-top-west-midlands-police-jobs/ accessed 25/11/2016
131)	ACC Michele Larmour, West Midlands Police
132)	ACC Michele Larmour, from Michele Larmour
133)	ACC Michele Larmour, West Midlands Police
134)	DCC Louisa Rolfe, West Midlands Police
135)	PC Maria McNeil and PC Georgina Oakley, response officers in Birmingham, from Steve Rice
136)	PCSO Kat Weir in Thames Valley Police, from Kat Weir
137)	Kat Weir, West Midlands Police
138)	Gail Arnold, West Midlands Police
139)	Alexandra Paxton, from Alexandra Paxton
140)	Sinead Cleaver, from Sinead Cleaver
141)	DCC Louisa Rolfe, West Midlands Police

Bibliography/Reference List:

---

[1] Letter to Birmingham Chief Constable from Bristol Chief Constable, 29th October 1920, Miss Dorothy Peto's file
[2] Birmingham Police Orders – 4th November 1839 – 18th June 1842
[3] Judicial Sub-Committee minutes, 21st October 1901, p389, 3456
[4] Finance and Fire Brigade Sub-Committee minutes, 11th February 1902, p391, 4424
[5] Finance and Fire Brigade Sub-Committee minutes, 25th March 1902, p397, 4470
[6] Judicial Sub-Committee minutes 11th July 1904, p68, 4,235
[7] Judicial Sub-Committee minutes 10th October 1904, p72, 4,274
[8] Finance and Fire Brigade Sub-Committee minutes 27th November 1914, 8937

[9] Police Orders 29th April 1918, p510
[10] http://news.bbc.co.uk/1/hi/england/lincolnshire/4610200.stm, accessed 22/11/2016
[11] 'Special' Watch Committee minutes 7th August 1914, in Watch Committee minutes 1914-1919, 5878
[12] The British Policewoman, Joan Lock, p77
[13] Judicial Sub-Committee minutes, 3rd February 1919, 8737 (attached letter from Home Office 24th January 1919, Ref 375, 227)
[14] Birmingham Post 23rd October 1914
[15] The British Policewoman, Joan Lock, 2014
[16] https://en.wikipedia.org/wiki/Margaret_Damer_Dawson accessed 22/10/2016
[17] The British Policewoman, Joan Lock,
[18] The Memoirs of Miss Dorothy Olivia Georgiana Peto OBE, Copyright Metropolitan Police Museum, published in 1993 by the Organising Committee for the European Conference on Equal Opportunities in the Police 1992 (referred to as Dorothy Peto memoirs, Met Police Museum in subsequent references)
[19] Letter from Chief Constable Rafter to Miss Florence Mildred White, 8th April 1925
[20] Great War Britain Birmingham 1914-1918 – Sian Roberts,
[21] Report of Miss N. Butchard, November 30th 1914, courtesy of the Metropolitan Women Police Association
[22] Patrol Committee organisers report from November 1914 to March 1915, courtesy of the Metropolitan Women Police Association
[23] NUWW, Birmingham Branch, Patrol Committee report for the week ending Jan 30th, courtesy of the Metropolitan Women Police Association
[24] Judicial Sub-Committee minutes 19th April 1915, 7655
[25] Judicial Sub-Committee 19th July 1915, 7757
[26] Great War Britain Birmingham Remembering 1914-1918, Sian Roberts in association with the Library of Birmingham
[27] Watch Committee minutes 3rd May 1916, 6269
[28] Judicial Sub-Committee Committee minutes 4th December 1916, 8093 & 8094. Confirmed in Watch Committee minutes 7th February 1917, 6411
[29] Great War Britain Birmingham 1914-1918, Sian Roberts
[30] Judicial Sub-Committee minutes 2nd April 1917, 8207
[31] Judicial Sub-Committee minutes 30th April 1917, 8204
[32] Judicial Sub-Committee minutes 14th May 1917, 8224-8226, Watch Committee minutes 14th May 1917, 6489-6491
[33] Watch Committee minutes 16th July 1917, 6555
[34] Watch Committee minutes 13th August 1917, 6565

[35] Judicial Sub-Committee minutes 1st October 1917, 8304
[36] Watch Committee minutes 9th October 1917, 6609
[37] Judicial Sub-Committee minutes 13th October 1917, 8335
[38] Wolverhampton City Archives DX-1008: Illuminated manuscript re: special constables ([1919]), detailed on https://wolverhamptonswar.wordpress.com/tag/women/ accessed 9/7/2018
[39] Walsall Observer 11th May 1918
[40] https://www.tearle.org.uk/roll-of-honour/war-stories-ww1/katherine-mary-tearle-1885-pioneer-of-the-wps/
[41] Policewomen – A History (2nd edition), Kerry Segrave, 2014
[42] Dorothy Peto memoirs, Met Police Museum
[43] Dorothy Peto memoirs, Met Police Museum
[44] The British Policewoman by Joan Lock, 1987
[45] Excerpt from the Baird Committee Report, quoted in The British Policewoman by Joan Lock
[46] Dorothy Peto memoirs, Met Police Museum
[47] The Baird Committee Report, referenced in The British Policewoman by Joan Lock
[48] PRO HO 45 11077, referenced in The British Policewoman by Joan Lock
[49] Dorothy Peto memoirs, Met Police Museum – when discussing her own appointment as an unattested officer in Birmingham
[50] Judicial Sub-Committee minutes 1st October 1917, (no page numbers) minute 8304
[51] Personnel ledger (c1900-1970) surnames beginning with 'C'
[52] Watch Committee Minutes 31/10/1931 (no page numbers) minute 6622
[53] Police Orders 26th April 1919, p708
[54] The Birmingham Post and Journal, Tuesday January 2nd 1940
[55] Book of reports by Sergeant Evelyn Miles to Chief Constable on the work of the Women's Police Department, WMP Museum
[56] Judicial Sub-Committee minutes 1st October 1917, 8309
[57] Judicial Sub-Committee minutes 3rd December 1917, 8349
[58] Watch Committee minutes 2nd January 1918, 6668
[59] Watch Committee minutes 25th October 1918, 10378
[60] Policing Birmingham: An Account of 150 years of Police in Birmingham, John W Reilly, 1989. Page 65.
[61] Second Report from the Select Committee on Distress from Want of Employment, 1895, accessed via http://www.newmanlocalhistory.org.uk/wp-content/uploads/history1-vol12.pdf on 2/11/2016
[62] Police Orders 1918 – 13th August 1918 page 142
[63] http://beta.charitycommission.gov.uk/charity-details/?regid=218497&subid=0 accessed 18/8/2016

[64] Judicial Sub-Committee minutes 1st July 1918, 8580

[65] Watch Committee minutes 3rd July 1918, 6852 & 6853

[66] Police Orders 31st March 1926, page 46 (1671)

[67] Police Orders 3rd October 1918, page 144, (2538)

[68] Judicial Sub-Committee minutes 27th October 1919, p87, 9059

[69] Wikipedia – Contagious Diseases Act - https://en.wikipedia.org/wiki/Contagious_Diseases_Acts Accessed 06:40 26/07/2016

[70] Police Orders 1918 3rd September page 178

[71] http://www.workhouses.org.uk/Birmingham/ accessed 20/8/2016

[72] Judicial Sub-Committee minutes 11th October 1920, p195, 9377

[73] Letter to Sir Leonard Dunning, H.M. Inspector of Constabulary 6th November 1920, Miss Dorothy Peto's personal file.

[74] The British Policewoman, Joan Lock, p132

[75] Judicial Sub-Committee minutes 22nd November 1920, p215, 9441

[76] Dorothy Peto Memoirs, Met Police Museum

[77] Judicial Sub-Committee minutes, 30th June 1922, p569, 705

[78] Judicial Sub-Committee minutes, 26th November 1924, p856 1510

[79] Judicial Sub-Committee minutes 11th May 1932, p189, 5357

[80] Judicial Sub-Committee minutes 1st March 1920, p123, 9183

[81] Judicial Sub-Committee minutes 29th March 1920, p133-134, 9207

[82] Salaries, Wages and Labour Committee minutes, 28th January 1921, p68, 1642, courtesy of Library of Birmingham

[83] Judicial Sub-Committee 28th January 1921, p260, 48

[84] Judicial Sub-Committee minutes 30th June 1922, p512, 577 & p545, 645

[85] Judicial Sub-Committee minutes, 10th January 1923, p606, 794

[86] Judicial Sub-Committee minutes 14th February 1923, p624, 820 & p625, 839

[87] Judicial Sub-Committee minutes, 14th March 1923, p643, 859 & p644, 890

[88] Judicial Sub-Committee minutes, 10th December 1924, p864, 1540

[89] The British Policewoman, Joan Lock, p166

[90] An Account of 150 years of Policing Birmingham, John Reilly, 1989. Page 65.

[91] Watch Committee Minutes 5th June 1929, page 187 (2818)

[92] Watch Committee Minutes 2nd October, p197, 2920

[93] Royal Commission on Police Powers and Procedure, 243, question 3667

[94] Royal Commission on Police Powers and Procedure, 235, question 7d

[95] Letter enquiring about vacancy in Birmingham Police, Florence White's personnel file. April 1925

[96] Letter to Florence White from Chief Constable Charles Haughton Rafter, dated 8/4/1925, in Florence White's personnel file

[97] Letter from Miss White to Chief Constable, 11th Feb 1937 in Florence White's personnel file

[98] Judicial Sub-Committee minutes, 15th April 1931, p53, 4884

[99] Watch Committee Minutes 2nd July 1930, p236, 4231

[100] Copy of Women Police Orders 29th October 1930, in Florence White's personnel file

[101] Adjustment of pay of women police, 7th November 1930, copy in Lucy Charlton's file

[102] Watch Committee Minutes, 3rd December 1930, p264, 4374

[103] Watch Committee Minutes, 30th July 1930, p243, 4268

[104] Judicial Sub-Committee minutes, 29th April 1931, p60, 4913

[105] Judicial Sub-Committee minutes, 14th October 1931, p118, 5113

[106] Birmingham City Police Orders 14th October 1931, 8pm dispatch, 18661

[107] Judicial Sub-Committee minutes 2nd December 1931, p139, 5979

[108] Judicial Sub-Committee minutes, 30th December 1931, p139, 5171

[109] Judicial Sub-Committee minutes, 6th April 1932, p177, 5315 & 27th April 1932, p184, 5329

[110] Letter in Ivy Dugard's personal file from Chief Constable to Superintendent Harrison, 1/1/1933

[111] Judicial Sub-Committee minutes 27th April 1932, p181, 5341 & 11th January 1933, p261, 5318

[112] Judicial Sub-Committee minutes 11th January 1933, p260-261, 5621

[113] Judicial Sub-Committee minutes 15th February 1933, p276, 5673

[114] Judicial Sub-Committee minutes 26th April 1933, p300-302, 5759

[115] Judicial Sub-Committee minutes 10th May 1933, p312, 5768

[116] Judicial Sub-Committee minutes 14th June 1933, p324, 5817

[117] Watch Committee minutes 5th July 1933, page 469 (5374)

[118] Judicial Sub-Committee minutes, 27th September 1933, p348, 5908

[119] Police Orders, 5th October 1933, p21222

[120] Police Orders, 23rd November 1933, p21408

[121] Watch Committee Minutes, 2nd July 1930, p240, 4213

[122] Police Orders, 6th December 1933, p21482

[123] Watch Committee Minutes, 23rd April 1934, p60

[124] Watch Committee Minutes 10th October 1934, 6440, p134 & 12th December 1934, p167

[125] Watch Committee Minutes 24th October 1934, 6477, p142

[126] Watch Committee Minutes 12th December 1934, 6551, p17

[127] Report in Susan Palmer's personnel file from Chief Constable Moriarty concerning the pay of Women Police

[128] The British Police, p145, referenced in The British Policewoman, Joan Lock
[129] Forty Years of Women's Work, 1917-1957, PA1269/7/1 – courtesy of the Herbert Art Gallery
[130] Coventry City Watch Committee Minutes, Sept 28th 1937, p1361
[131] Report of the Police Women to the Coventry City Watch Committee – 14th November 1939, courtesy of Herbert Art Gallery
[132] Obituary of Ena Goodacre, which appeared in The Times March 17th 2008 and the NRA Journal Summer 2008
[133] Dudley Council Watch Committee Minutes, 50/ No.12 Minutes 1934-44, 13 December 1939 (113/72)

[134] Dudley Council Watch Committee Minutes, 50/ No.12 Minutes 1934-44, 9 October 1940 (645/123)

[135] Dudley Council Watch Committee Minutes, 50/ No.12 Minutes 1934-44, 19 March 1941 (264/147) & 10 September 1941 (541/180)

[136] Watch Committee Judicial Sub-Committee minutes 27th July 1933 5881 p342
[137] Extract from Watch Committee report November 1965, file of Marjorie Lewis, West Midlands Police Museum
[138] Policing Birmingham: An Account of 150 years of Police in Birmingham, p96, John W Reilly, 1989
[139] Policing Birmingham: An Account of 150 years of Police in Birmingham, John W Reilly, 1989
[140] Policing Birmingham: An Account of 150 years of Police in Birmingham, John W Reilly, 1989
[141] http://hansard.millbanksystems.com/written_answers/1945/nov/08/police-auxiliaries-release accessed 22/9/2016
[142] Police Orders 29th March 1946, p38451
[143] National Council of Women, Coventry Branch, letter to Mrs Home Peel from Miss Amy Baker, Secretary, 20/3/1941. Courtesy of Metropolitan Women Police Association.
[144] Letter from Chief Constable Edwin Tilley, Wolverhampton Borough Police, to Mrs Home Peel 7th July 1941, courtesy of the Metropolitan Women Police Association.
[145] Police Orders, 8th February 1946, p38377
[146] Police Orders 31st July 1946, 38643
[147] Birmingham Mail, 17th June 1957
[148] Report from Supt Norah Gray, 16th May 1957, in Agnes Tantrum's personal file
[149] Policing Birmingham: An Account of 150 years of Police in Birmingham, John W Reilly, 1989

[150] Birmingham Mail, Thursday 30th March 1950

[151] Policing Birmingham: An Account of 150 years of Police in Birmingham, John W Reilly, 1989

[152] Report to Superintendent Bloomer, 11th March 1944 in Jeanie Law's personal file

[153] Letter from Chief Constable Dodd to Jeanie Law, 11th May 1962, Jeanie Law's personal file

[154] http://history.west-midlands.police.uk/tag/schipper/

[155] Sunday Mercury, 14th April 1963

[156] Birmingham Mail 8th April 1957

[157] Barbara Denis de Vitre, 1929, woman police, the Felican, p29, referenced in '150 years of HMIC'

[158] The History of Her Majesty's Inspectorate of Constabulary – the first 150 years (1856-2006) by Richard Cowley and Peter Todd, 2006

[159] http://www.westmidlandspolicemuseum.co.uk/wmconstabulary.htm, accessed 23/10/2016

[160] Policing Birmingham: An Account of 150 years of Police in Birmingham, John W Reilly, 1989

[161] http://www.police.govt.nz/angela-harwood-qsm

[162] Policing Birmingham: An Account of 150 years of Police in Birmingham, John W Reilly, 1989

[163] Including Birmingham City & West Midlands Constabulary files, Walsall and Wolverhampton ledgers held in the museum. Excluding WAPC, lock-up matrons and civilian staff.

[164] http://www.west-midlands.police.uk/latest-news/news.aspx?id=3679 accessed 24/11/2016

[165] http://www.dailymail.co.uk/femail/article-481882/Condemned-virgins-The-million-women-robbed-war.html accessed 5/11/2016

[166] Women in Love Without Men, Laura Gillan, Express and Star, Monday 9th February 1970

[167] http://hansard.millbanksystems.com/written_answers/1974/may/03/west-midlands-police, HC Deb 03 May 1974 vol 872 c263W 263W

[168] http://www.voice-online.co.uk/article/west-midlands-first-black-police-woman accessed 1/9/2016

[169] West Midlands Police Newsbeat magazine, September 1991

[170] http://news.bbc.co.uk/1/hi/england/coventry_warwickshire/4847506.stm accessed 30/10/2016

[171] https://www.gloucestershire.police.uk/more-on-us/about-us/chief-officer-group/ accessed 9/10/2016

[172] http://www.westmidlands-pcc.gov.uk/transparency/bob-jones-archive/2014-bob-jones-news-archive/women-lead-the-way-in-top-west-midlands-police-jobs/ accessed 8/10/2016

[173] http://www.independent.co.uk/news/uk/female-ruc-officers-to-be-armed-david-mckittrick-reports-on-moves-to-extend-equality-of-opportunity-1460552.html

[174] Workforce Strategy Bulletin Report, 1st August 2016, West Midlands Police

A Fair Cop: 1917 – 2017
The trail blazing policewomen of Birmingham & the West Midlands

From the pioneer policewomen recruited during the First World War to full integration across roles and ranks, this book documents the journeys, struggles and achievements of policewomen across the West Midlands since Evelyn Miles and Rebecca Lipscombe became the first female officers in the region, in Birmingham in 1917.

Thanks to the vast amount of records that have been preserved not only in the West Midlands Police Museum, but also those from other museums and libraries across the West Midlands, it has been possible to outline various different female firsts in policing throughout the region. Thanks to some dedicated research by our volunteers, we have been able to also tell the stories of the first female officers in Walsall, Wolverhampton, Coventry and Dudley, and highlight changes to policy and policing in general through the decades.

Let us take you on a journey from the early days of policing in the 1800s right up to modern times, sharing some incredible and inspirational personal stories on the way and including many original images that have not previously been published.

ISBN 9780995706118

9 780995 706118